1984

SELF-HELP WORKS

SELF-HELP WORKS

by
Edward W. O'Rourke

Bishop of Peoria

PAULIST PRESS
New York/Ramsey/Toronto

Library of Congress
Catalog Card Number: 78-56967

ISBN: 0-8091-2147-6

Cover Design: George Wuellner

Published by Paulist Press
Editorial Office: 1865 Broadway, New York, N.Y. 10023
Business Office: 545 Island Road, Ramsey, N.J. 07446

Printed and bound in the
United States of America

Contents

Peter Hunting
died at age 24 in Vietnam on November 12, 1965

Michael Murphy
died at age 22 in Laos on January 25, 1966

Max Sinkler
died at age 25 in Vietnam on April 27, 1966

Frederick Cheydleur
died at age 20 in Laos on March 25, 1967

Martin Clish
died at age 27 in Laos on April 6, 1967

David Gitelson
died at age 25 in Vietnam on January 25, 1968

Chandler Edwards
died at age 23 in Laos on April 24, 1969

Dennis Mummert
died at age 23 in Laos on August 5, 1969

Arthur Stillman
died at age 27 in Laos on August 5, 1969

Alexander Shimkin
died at age 18 in Vietnam on July 14, 1972

Introduction

Self-help—as presented in this book—is a technique employed in economic and social development programs whereby those needing development help themselves. They have ultimate control of the programs. Programs are truly devised to meet their felt needs. Those who provide assistance from outside attempt to complement the resources of the local population, making available materials, money and skills which the local population lack and without which the programs would either fail or be less effective.

This type of self-help is not an entirely new technique. For more than one hundred years cooperatives and credit unions have provided extremely effective structures through which low-income people can improve their income and their control over their economic and social destinies.[1] Early in the nineteenth century a group of weavers at Rochdale, England, devised what we now call the Rochdale Principles of Cooperation, which embody a marvelously effective and amazingly democratic manner in which a group of people with common interests can engage cooperatively in production, consumption and credit.

The Rochdale Principles are as follows:

1. Open membership. No one will be arbitrarily excluded from a cooperative.

2. Political and religious neutrality. Members are permitted to join religious or political groups of their choice.

3. Democratic control. Each member has one vote without regard to the number of shares he owns.

4. Limited returns to capital. These returns shall not exceed the minimum prevailing rate of interest.

5. Earnings are distributed to patrons on the basis of their patronage. The one who buys the most from the cooperative receives the greatest patronage dividend.

6. A portion of earnings shall be spent for education of members and nonmembers.

7. Business shall be done for cash.

8. Current market prices shall be charged.

9. Where possible, cooperatives shall combine their strength in federations for the purpose of wholesaling, manufacturing and providing services too large to be undertaken by individual cooperatives.

These tested principles of cooperation have been further expanded and refined so that they can be applied to economic and social development on larger scales. More will be said about these principles of self-help in chapter 1.

Unions, too, are tested means whereby people can help themselves. During the latter part of the nineteenth century, modern craft and industrial unions began to emerge in Western Europe and the United States. Through such unions workers gain a significant degree of control over their income, working conditions and other aspects of their economic life.[2]

On May 15, 1891, Pope Leo XIII published his encyclical "On the Condition of Labor," in which he clearly affirmed the right of workers to form unions for the purpose of collective bargaining. In 1931 Pope Pius XI, in his encyclical "Forty Years After," reaffirmed that right to organize and pointed to the benefits to management, labor and society that had resulted from Pope Leo's encyclical.

In chapter 4 a summary will be made of the efforts by Cesar Chavez and agricultural workers of California to utilize unionization as one of the instruments for the uplift of extremely poor farm workers.

In the years from 1955 to 1970 the self-help approach to economic-social problems of disadvantaged persons in the United States and in the Third World was extensively employed and significantly improved. One of the reasons for the emergence of this new emphasis was the fact that from 1946 to 1955, particularly in the United States, there had been an excessive turning to the opposite of self-help, namely doing things for and to people and pushing upon them self-demeaning handouts.

The United States emerged from World War II the most powerful and the most prosperous nation in the history of the world. Moreover, the leaders and people of this nation were convinced of some kind of "manifest destiny" whereby they were called to solve the economic, social and political problems of the world whether or not local populations desired such remedies. The impressive success of our efforts to help rebuild Western Europe and Japan after World War II convinced us that our technology, financial institutions and attitude were precisely what the world—particularly those unfortunate people living in poverty in the Third World—needed.[3] This philosophy was prominent in agencies of the U.S. government, particularly the U.S. Agency for International Development (at one time called Point IV). Under these programs American agriculturists, engineers, educators, financiers, and so forth, moved into Third World communities and did things the American way. Although there was usually the necessary cooperation of the local governmental officials, the people most directly affected were seldom considered or consulted.

In the meanwhile, the American people with their uncommon generosity responded to the hunger that prevailed in much of the world after World War II with immense contributions of food and other necessities. Not only agencies of government, but private agencies such as Church World Service (CWS) and Catholic Relief Services (CRS) delivered staggering amounts of American agricultural and industrial products into various nations of the world. Although sincere efforts were made to avoid corruption in the distribution of these goods and to bring them to those who needed them most, very little thought was given to the impact handouts had on the self-respect and initiative of the recipients. Eventually it became evident that, after the emergency had passed, any continuation of handouts was more harmful than helpful. In Third World nations the easy availability of relief supplies served as an obstacle to development of the productivity of the local people.

In 1958 the American public was rudely awakened to the shortcomings of its overseas assistance policies by books such as *The Ugly American* by William J. Lederer and Eugene Burdick. Lederer and Burdick pointed out the negative features of American relief and development programs abroad but also featured, in the person of Homer Atkins, a better way of dealing with some of these problems. Homer in this book was the "chicken man" who lived among the villagers of Sarkhon and helped them improve the quality of their flocks. Many of us engaged in self-help programs recognized in Homer Atkins a striking similarity to the personality and work of a certain "Pop Buehl" who had served in similar capacities for many years in Laos.

Thus the stage was set for a new emphasis on self-help. It is interesting to note that the response to this challenge came chiefly from private organizations. Apparently they were much more adaptable than the larger and more bureaucratic agencies of government. For example, CRS pioneered Food for Work Programs in many Third World nations. Instead of donating food outright, grain, milk and other commodities were used as partial payment of wages for workers on roads, irrigation systems and other public works. By 1977, CRS was devoting $36 million per year to such programs.

It was my privilege during this period to work very closely with several of the self-help organizations that had a tremendous impact on development at home and abroad. Chapter 2 through 12 are descriptions of the policies and personalities in nine of these organizations. It is important that there be an accurate record of the spectacular successes of these organizations in human development and the many instances of their solid economic accomplishments. In our own times an increasing number of leaders in government and in the private sector are beginning to toy with other techniques that experience has proved to be vastly less effective and less desirable. It is my sincere hope that this book will help persons in such positions to know more accurately the alternatives that have been tested in the past.

This description of self-help is first and foremost a description of marvelous people—not only those Americans who provided leadership in the above-mentioned nine organizations, but also a much larger number of people in the communities at home and abroad that adopted self-help programs. Almost without exception all of these people were men and women of vision, great generosity and unbelievable perseverance. The American leaders include such magnificent personalities as Monsignor Luigi Ligutti and Stanley Andrews of International Voluntary Services; Father Albert McKnight and Miss Una Mae Hargrave of Southern Consumers Cooperative; Marie Cirillo and Ben Poage of the Commission on Religion in Appalachia; and Cesar Chavez and Delores Huerta of the United Farm Workers Organization.

Among the most magnificent personalities I have ever met are those who responded in the communities at home and abroad where self-help programs were initiated. These include the North Vietnamese priest who led his people in the village of St. Vincent's (twenty miles north of Saigon) in building a very complete village with comfortable homes, school and church; the illiterate blacks of southwest Louisiana who, through Southern Consumers Cooperative, became confident and articulate leaders; scores of Appalachian men and women who formed effective pig, rabbit, vegetable and handicraft cooperatives; and the thousands of agricultural workers who exposed themselves to great bodily harm and near starvation for several years in their effort to establish the United Farm Workers Organization.

A third very large group of persons provided indispensable support to self-help programs at home and abroad, namely, the thousands of volunteers who have served in these projects. Most of the volunteers were young men and women, aged twenty through thirty, who devoted themselves to self-help programs with a generosity seldom paralleled. Their willingness to live with the local population and to respect their culture, religion and initiatives was indispensable to the success of the programs we are describing.

I am most grateful to the present leadership of the above-mentioned self-help organizations who have so generously made available information and records without which much of this book would have been impossible.

1
The Why and How of Self-Help

The *why* of self-help is first and foremost based upon the right of every human being to self-esteem and to a reasonable control over his or her destiny. Self-esteem is badly eroded when a person is forced by hunger or other circumstance repeatedly to stand in soup lines or other places in which handouts are given. Such a person quickly assumes a position of inferiority in relationship to those who are giving to him. The handout represents only a very temporary solution to his problems. Such a person progressively loses control over his future and that of his family.[4]

So also the local population is humiliated and demeaned when outsiders take control of development projects. Surely those who are most directly affected have the right to exercise initiative and ultimate control in such programs. Embodied in such practice is the assumption that the outsider is vastly superior to the local population. Such assumptions are seldom verified. In the self-help programs described in chapters 2 to 11 it becomes apparent that, given the proper opportunity, leaders of extraordinary skill and perseverance emerge in most local populations.

This concern for human dignity takes on special

urgency among Christians. We Christians are committed to a religion according to which others are our brothers and sisters in Christ and deserve great love and respect. Any affront to the dignity and self-esteem of a fellow Christian is a violation of a most basic religious principle.[5]

The second *why* for self-help is the fact that it is vastly more effective than the opposite approach to economic, political and social development. In self-help programs a staggering amount of local energy and resources is released. Most outside agents of change are prepared to offer only a fraction of the resources needed for development programs and that over a very limited period of time. Unless the much greater human and natural resources of the local population are tapped, such development programs are destined for failure.

It is true that the self-help approach is sometimes slower than that of a program in which outsiders do things their way and according to their preferences. However, in the long run, self-help programs are vastly more efficient ways of using the resources available to accomplish enduring results.

In such self-help programs the greatest product is human development. While both the local people and the outside agents of change are working together on a specific economic, educational or other project, the local people are gaining immensely in development skills, self-confidence and experience in working together. In most instances this human development dwarfs in significance the economic, social and political goals reached.

The "how" of self-help can be expressed in the following five principles. These principles will be illustrated and vindicated in chapters 2 through 11. Experience shows that observing these principles greatly enhances the likelihood of success in self-help programs.

Preserve Local Initiative and Control

Those who are most directly affected by social and economic problems should be those who retain initiative and control of any development program. When outside agents of change attempt to arrogate to themselves these prerogatives, they are almost always met with suspicion and resistance. These outside agents of change can best serve the program by creating a situation in which the local people will become more consciously aware of their problems and of the resources with which they might deal with those problems. As plans for action on such problems develop, it will become apparent precisely what outside material resources, skills and financial help are needed. The outsider can tactfully suggest possible solutions to problems and help the local people evaluate the probable consequences of various lines of action.

An essential feature of this progress is the setting of priorities. I recall an instance in a development effort in Yucatan, Mexico, in which we outside agents of change presumed that the first priority should be an irrigation system. Much to our amazement, the local people determined first to refurbish the city plaza. A moment of reflection makes it clear why they chose to do so. Their families gathered at the city plaza almost every evening to relax. The cathedral and many of the shops of the city were located around that plaza. It represented a very important feature of their culture. Incidentally, after completing the plaza refurbishing, the local people proceeded with the irrigation project that we outsiders thought so important. Had we attempted to interfere with their priorities, they would certainly have rejected us.

Not every person is capable of acting as an outside agent of change in a development project. Such persons must be prepared humbly to respect the culture, religion and outlook of the native people and their leaders. Moreover, if the outsider lacks true respect for the native population, this fact will be recognized and the effectiveness of such outsiders will be greatly undermined. Those planning to act as agents of change in a Third World country should prepare with a diligent study of the religion, culture and other special features of the people whom they propose to serve. Gaining reasonable skills in the local language is one of the several ways in which we show respect for such persons. An agent of change would do well to practice listening. Most Americans are much too quick in offering their opinions and giving directives.

Serve Low-Income People

In most developing countries and to a somewhat lesser degree in our own nation, the already rich and powerful are inclined to respond quickly to new technology or other kinds of assistance. If this occurs, the result is a worsening of the socio-economic situation. It is imperative, therefore, that self-help programs be made truly available to those who are poor and powerless.

Since the wealthy and powerful have vastly more

influence on their governments than do the poor, an agent of change must very tactfully avoid subordinating the project to local governmental officials. On the other hand, it is neither appropriate nor feasible to pursue development projects in a Third World nation without minimal approval of the local government. Many extremely fine development programs have been abandoned precisely because the local government was either ineffectual or corrupt or both. In order that an agent of change may effectively influence low-income people, it is usually necessary for him to live among them at an economic level not significantly different from theirs. It is precisely for this reason that volunteers and missionaries are often the most effective agents of change. Many governmental officials are either incapable or unwilling to reach the poor and powerless effectively.

In the early stages of the "Green Revolution," the new varieties of rice were made available to relatively small farmers in portions of Southeast Asia and Africa. For example, Catholic Relief Services provided in Southeast Asia a packet, costing approximately $75, that contained a quantity of the new rice seed, appropriate amounts of fertilizer and insecticide, and the assurance that the essential technical assistance needed to implement the program would be available. Similarly the International Voluntary Services became deeply involved in promoting the use of these new varieties of rice among the low-income people of Vietnam and Laos. In those nations in which the wealthier growers adopted this new agricultural technology and the small farmers didn't, the condition of the latter became immensely worse. By reason of the great increase in productivity of the new variety of rice, the per-unit price fell sharply at local markets. Those following the old technology found their income severely reduced.

Utilize Intermediate Technology

If we seriously intend to make new technology available to low-income people, that technology must not be too complex or too costly. It is foolish to attempt to move from extremely simple technology to complex and costly technology in a single step.[6] For example, in parts of Indonesia farmers are still plowing their ground by hand with sticks. The obvious next step would not be a costly tractor but a shovel, which would greatly improve the productivity of each worker. If we pursue intermediate technology, it is likely that the local people will be able to sustain and build on it after outside help has ceased. In order that this may be true, it is important to introduce only that type of equipment which can be repaired and replaced with the resources at the disposal of the local people. For example, some of the most effective irrigation projects have been developed with local materials such as bamboo, palm leaves, parts of bicycles, and so forth. In light of the limited supply of petroleum products and the rapidly increasing costs of the same, great caution should be exercised in initiating any kind of development that relies heavily on the use of petroleum products.

Consider Integral Development

Unless the several interrelated economic features are simultaneously improved, no development project is likely to endure. Agricultural production, improved transportation, educational advances, creation of credit for low-income people, and so forth, must be simultaneously pursued. During the 1960s I observed in Laos a rapid increase of rice production by reason of the new rice varieties at a time in which storage facilities for this increased production were not available and transportation of surplus rice to places where it was needed was very nearly impossible. In some instances, such rice was carried in a sack on the back of a man. En route to his destination, this man would consume half of the rice he was carrying. Obviously, significant agricultural development is not possible unless these related aspects of development are also considered.

The education and leadership formation that makes possible one form of development could rather quickly bear fruit in other types of development as well. For example, we attempt in Third World countries and in poor neighborhoods in the United States to develop simultaneously credit unions and two or more types of cooperatives. The basic organizational structure and membership participation is similar in all forms of cooperatives. When the Commission on Religion in Appalachia began to respond to the needs of people in Central Appalachia in the late 1960s, a whole series of cooperatives quickly emerged. In many instances a husband would be engaged in a pig producers' cooperative while his wife was a member of a handicraft cooperative. This represents a great economy of effort and a further guarantee of success.

Sustain Projects Until Viable

Most development efforts require approximately

ten years to establish. Those agents of change who initiate projects and then abandon them before they become viable add to the problems of the local population. Unfortunately, almost all government-supported programs tend to be of short duration. Changes of political parties and other basic political facts of life cause this unfortunate trend. For this reason, nongovernmental organizations have a much better track record in promoting development projects than do agencies of government. Among the several reasons why missionaries are relatively effective in such undertakings is the fact that they tend to remain in a given area for many years. This makes it possible for them to continue assistance until the local population is truly able to completely manage the project.

One of the most difficult features of development is the creation of management skills among the local population. Quite frequently the outside agent of change must assume a management role in the early stages of a cooperative or other development project. He should immediately surround himself with counterparts— promising local leaders—to whom he will convey all the information and skill that he possesses. When these local leaders are able to take over management, it is time for the outsider to move on.

Keeping these principles of self-help in mind, let us now recount the struggles and accomplishments of several American-based organizations that have advanced self-help significantly at home and abroad.

2
Southern Consumers Cooperative

Southern Consumers Cooperative (SCC), founded in 1962 in southwestern Louisiana, differs in several significant ways from typical American farmers' cooperatives. SCC was formed by and serves the needs of desperately poor southern blacks. Most other agricultural cooperatives are operated by relatively prosperous whites. The special needs of its members caused SCC to organize, in addition to their cooperative, several small enterprises and a major financial institution, as we shall see later.

Recent experience indicates that cooperatives not only make modest contributions to the economic welfare of low-income people; they provide an even more valuable service in helping to restore self-respect, initiative and hope among these people.

Poverty alone, though undesirable, is not unbearable. History is filled with illustrations of poor people who have lived happy, fruitful lives. My grandparents lived extremely poorly in Ireland in the early 19th century. Yet, they retained a high degree of dignity, diligence and refinement.

Most of the American poor experience alienation as well as poverty. They feel that they have been excluded from ownership of property, proprietorship in business and the role of decision maker in civil affairs. Accepting such a position is destructive of self-respect and cannot be reconciled with the deep-rooted aspirations of mankind.

Cooperatives can help remedy both poverty and alienation. This has been demonstrated during recent years in many cooperatives serving people in low-income areas. Many of the members of these cooperatives gain through their membership their first experience in democracy and self-determination. It is difficult to fully appreciate the great significance of such experiences. They pave the way for fuller participation in voting, church activities and the affairs of the community. They help dispel self-hatred, which is at the root of much antisocial activity.

Father Albert J. McKnight, a black member of the Holy Ghost Order, born in Brooklyn, is the founder of Southern Consumers Cooperative. In 1957 he was assigned to serve as pastor to two small Roman Catholic congregations in Kaplan and Abbeyville, Louisiana. Since more than two-thirds of his parishioners were illiterate, Father McKnight rather logically concluded that a literacy school was indicated. After two years of valiant effort in this direction, he found that there were more teachers than students in his school.

At this point Father McKnight observed one of the fundamental principles of self-help, namely, to listen to the people concerned and to respond to their felt needs. After extensive listening, he concluded that the people's first concern was for an improvement of their economic condition. While they were so desperately poor and hungry, all other services seemed insignificant.

During the summer of 1960, Father McKnight

learned more about cooperatives and the Rochdale Principles at St. Francis University, Nova Scotia. He returned to his parishes in southwestern Louisiana and immediately began the process of forming a cooperative to help the people with their economic needs. Knowing of my interest in cooperatives, he invited me to join him in this effort from time to time. Later, I was able to serve as an advocate for SCC when they sought loans and grants from federal agencies. Valuable assistance was also provided by Miss Una Mae Hargrave, a member of the Grail, a community of Roman Catholic women committed to educational and social service programs.

Over a two-year period, Father McKnight, Miss Hargrave and other local leaders explained to low-income residents of the area the advantages of membership in the proposed cooperative. From the outset, they determined that the people should help themselves. The first block of capital employed by SCC was raised by the impoverished members themselves at the rate of $12.50 per month. As soon as a family had invested $300 in SCC, it became a full-fledged member thereof. By 1962 SCC had gained a total of 2,000 members. In 1964 it was the beneficiary of one of the very first loans made by the Office of Economic Opportunity. That loan, amounting to $25,000, together with the capital raised through membership contributions, enabled SCC to establish a loan company and a fruit cake factory. The loan company provided the same essential services as a credit union. The fruit cake factory, located at St. Charles, Louisiana, produced a very high quality fruit cake called "Acadian Delight." Both of these operations of SCC continue until this time and have been the foundation of the cooperative's economic endeavors.

In 1965 Southern Consumers Educational Foundation (SCEF) was created. It received a $1,000,000 federal grant to establish Head Start programs for the poor children of the region. SCEF continues to this time, engaging now in more modest endeavors such as tutorial programs and granting of scholarships. Members of SCC found that local white-dominated financial institutions would not make loans to them. Therefore they resolved to provide their own major capital institution, which was called Southern Cooperative Development Fund, Inc. (SCDF). Begun in 1969, it accumulated assets of $89,000 by 1970; in July 1976 the total assets had reached $7,027,379. During 1975–1976 SCDF made ninety-nine loans to forty-two cooperatives and small enterprises in nine states. One of the major financial supporters of SCDF has been the Ford Foundation.

SCC and the several cooperatives and small enterprises that have branched out from it have added significantly to the income of their members. For example, prior to the formation of the Grand Marie Sweet Potato Cooperative, local black farmers received approximately $.25 per pound from local buyers for their sweet potatoes. Once the cooperative was fully operative, their returns reached $3.25 per pound. Similarly, during the year ending July 30, 1975, the Mana-Hill Farmers Cooperative processed tomatoes that sold for over $650,000. Included among the several enterprises financed by SCDF are the Northern Bolivar County Farmer Cooperative, which is engaged in a 748-acre farming operation, producing 225 acres of rice, 500 acres of soy beans and 23 acres of wheat. The project's gross income for 1976 was $122,850. Similarly, the Petit Jean Agricultural Corporation, located in Ville Platte, Louisiana, operates a 600-acre commercial farm. Petit Jean is growing 50 acres of sweet potatoes,

50 acres of cabbage and 500 acres of soy beans. Included among the organizations assisted by SCDF are several grocery cooperatives, a land and equipment leasing cooperative, several fishing cooperatives, a rabbit-growing cooperative and a land-buying association.

Undoubtedly the greatest fruit of SCC has been the uplift it has exercised on the outlook and capabilities of many of its members. For example, during the early 1960s Carolyn Zippert, a teenager, joined SCC. From this experience she became keenly interested in rural development. Eventually she earned a master's degree in Rural Social Development at Louisiana State University and observed rural development later in Turkey as an exchange student. She is now employed at a cooperative health unit in Epps, Alabama.

Consider the case of Alfred McZeal. Back in 1964, he was working at $42.00 per week as a porter in a five-and-ten-cent store. When the store closed, Alfred became involved in SCC and worked his way up to the position of general manager of SCC, directing a staff of twenty persons. Alfred, Carolyn and hundreds of other members of SCC have become vastly more articulate and confident by reason of their leadership roles in this organization, which is truly theirs.

Opposition to SCC by local white leaders was severe at the beginning. Back in the 1960s, southern whites were not cordial to any organization that would make blacks economically independent. There have also been internal troubles in SCC. In a few cases employees proved either incompetent or dishonest. Some of the cooperatives started eventually failed. Still, throughout it all, Father McKnight and his associates have manifested a marvelous perseverance.

21

Father McKnight believes that cooperatives are not the ultimate solution to the economic and social problems of blacks. These problems are too huge and too deeply rooted to be solved by one structure. On the other hand, there can be no doubt that the human development effected by SCC and its associate companies is an immense step toward preparing blacks of the South for whatever future steps are needed in order that they may enjoy economic justice, political freedom and social opportunity.

3
Cooperatives Bloom in Appalachia

During the 1960s cooperatives and other locally owned enterprises sprang up in many Appalachian communities. The catalysts for much of this development were religious leaders, particularly those associated with the Commission on Religion in Appalachia (CORA), an ecumenical organization.

Poverty in Appalachia is due largely to a rape of natural resources by outside individuals and corporations and to the human erosion that necessarily followed. For several generations, trainloads of coal and other minerals have been shipped out of Appalachia to provide energy and wealth to people in other states. Industrialists have polluted most of the rivers and streams of the area and denuded many of the forests.[7]

Human erosion is apparent everywhere in Appalachia. For several generations the younger, more capable people of Appalachia have migrated to other areas. Lack of adequate education and malnutrition have badly affected the spirit of the people. There is abundant evidence of a tragic poverty of spirit and loss of hope in most Appalachian communities. Many of the houses built by the mining companies reflect a poverty culture—few windows, no paint, no bathrooms, and so forth.

Appalachia differs from other poverty areas in the world in that it is surrounded by some of the most affluent communities of our entire nation. To the east are the great industrial cities; to the south are Atlanta, Birmingham and other prosperous cities; to the north is the prosperous Great Lakes area and to the west, the great agricultural communities of the Midwest.

The Appalachian Redevelopment Act of 1965 represented a massive effort by our federal government to provide the basis for economic and social growth in that region. This act provided for the construction of roads, schools, water systems, sewerage disposal systems and other public facilities, which hopefully would make a better life for the local people and attract industry and tourists from the surrounding regions.

Prior to 1960 the weakest link in programs for the redevelopment of Appalachia was found at the local level. There had been too little leadership by the Appalachian people themselves at the community level. Most of the economic and social institutions of the area were extremely ineffectual. Even the churches of Appalachia had relatively little impact upon these issues, because most of the Appalachian people live for the next world. Their religious services help to distract them from the miseries in which they find themselves.

CORA, a coalition of seventeen denominations in Appalachia and ten state Councils of Churches, was organized in 1965. CORA is served by a two-level staff that has proven extremely effective. First, a small full-time staff is based in CORA's headquarters in Knoxville, Tennessee; this staff plans and coordinates the overall program. Second, a "collegiate staff" of men and women are provided by the member denominations and supported by them. This collegiate staff devotes from 30 to 100 percent of its time to CORA. This permits CORA to have a much larger staff in service in Appalachia without greatly increasing overhead costs, and it makes the response of CORA to local needs quick and effective. It also eliminates the inefficient arrangement in which staff people are at certain times not fully engaged in any meaningful work.

From the beginning, CORA has sought to redefine the mission of the Church in Appalachia so that it could most effectively minister to the region's peculiar needs. This resulted very quickly in a heavy emphasis by CORA on human development and self-determination. Since one of the biggest challenges to CORA was to motivate local church members, the self-help approach to practical economic and social problems immediately became a very big part of the CORA program.

Back in 1968, CORA formed a self-help task force and invited me to serve as its chairman. We in the self-help task force resolved to follow the basic principle of self-help, namely that we would listen to the local people and try to respond to their felt needs. Accordingly, we convened local Appalachian leaders at a listening meeting at Morehead State University Campus, Morehead, Kentucky, during the winter of 1968. After three days we emerged understanding very clearly that these Appalachian leaders considered the forming and strengthening of cooperatives and other small enterprises a top priority. In an effort to implement these objectives, our task force sponsored and conducted a series of three cooperatives' workshops in Kentucky, West Virginia and North Carolina. Approximately three hundred fifty Appalachian grass-roots leaders attended these workshops. Most of them went

25

back to their communities prepared to strengthen and improve existing cooperatives or to take the initial steps toward the formation of cooperatives.

In my capacity both as chairman of the self-help task force and as one of the several "collegiate" staff members of CORA, I spent approximately two months each year for the next four years visiting Appalachian communities in which these cooperatives were being formed. At each community I would help the local leaders ascertain precisely where they stood in the task of making a cooperative viable and then help them to take the next step forward. The response of the local people was cordial and extremely positive.

We quickly realized that an ongoing agency was necessary to provide managerial, financial and other services to these struggling new cooperatives. We found already in existence an excellent example of such an organization, The Grass Roots Economic Development Corporation, Inc. (GREDC), at Jackson, Kentucky. We were able to channel to GREDC additional funds and some of our collegiate staff personnel. They proceeded then to serve various cooperatives and other community organizations with technical assistance, feasibility studies of projects and various managerial and bookkeeping services. The Reverend Ben Poage was one of the full-time staff members at GREDC. He quickly emerged as one of the most capable and dedicated of the churchmen serving self-help projects in Appalachia.

Realizing the value of GREDC and knowing the special talents of Ben Poage, CORA's self-help task force proceeded to form a new organization called Human/Economic Appalachian Development (HEAD Corporation). HEAD is a coalition of groups such as

GREDC making the above-mentioned managerial and technical services available to communities in addition to Jackson, Kentucky. HEAD Corporation continues to grow in effectiveness. It provides services to a very large number of cooperatives and small industries throughout Central Appalachia.

Among the fruits of these efforts was a rapid increase in numbers and in effectiveness of handicraft cooperatives. This is due in part to the fact that there has been a long tradition of handicraft making in many Appalachian communities. With assistance from the CORA self-help task force and HEAD, a very effective federation of handicraft cooperatives was formed. One of the services of this federation is the marketing of handicrafts on a cooperative basis. One of the major thrusts in this direction is operation MATCH. Nina Poage, the wife of Ben, is director of marketing for this corporation, which is based in Berea, Kentucky. MATCH publishes a handsome catalogue of handicrafts produced in Appalachia. It is now sponsoring a project called the "Living Catalogue." In this project, trunks are filled with assortments of handicrafts and shipped to various county fairs and other gatherings where such products might be sold. Each trunk is accompanied by a representative of MATCH who displays the handicrafts and takes orders.

Cooperatives and small enterprises that have grown up by reason of the above-mentioned church-related agencies include the Producers' Cooperatives for Handicraft, Feeder Pig, Rabbit and Vegetable Producers; consumers' cooperatives such as grocery stores; and small industries that manufacture furniture, molasses and wood products.

It should also be noted that a significant input into

these many efforts has been derived from young people who volunteer their services for a few weeks or a few years. The Reverend Ralph Beiting of the Christian Appalachian Project, Lancaster, Kentucky, has been especially effective in enlisting, training and counseling volunteers of this sort.

Over a decade has passed since these initial steps were made toward the formation of cooperatives and small industries in Central Appalachia. The vast majority of these organizations are still flourishing, a tribute to the soundness with which they were planned and initiated. The increased economic resources that have resulted from these cooperatives and enterprises is substantial. Vastly more precious, however, is the human development that has resulted. A whole new attitude and outlook is emerging in many of these Appalachian communities. Prior to 1960 most commentaries about Appalachia were characterized by a note of hopelessness. Books on this topic bore ominous titles such as *Yesterday's People* and *Night Comes to the Cumberlands*.[8] Recent developments in this region warrant a different type of report, perhaps "A New Day Dawns in Appalachia."

4
Ownership and Income

All real wealth, that is, goods and services, is produced either by labor (the human factor in production) or by capital (land, structures and machines, the nonhuman factor in production). Consequently, all income is derived ultimately from either capital or labor.

Technological advances in agriculture, industry and business are bringing about a steady increase in the relative contribution of capital to the production of goods and services and a corresponding reduction in the relative contribution of labor to the same. Costly machines, including computers, are replacing workers or greatly reducing the role of workers.

An obvious implication of this trend is the need for more widespread ownership of capital. A growing number of people should derive a substantial part of their income from ownership. Then the reduction of labor requirements in our agriculture, industry and business would result in more leisure for our people, but would not either cause a decrease in their income or prompt them to demand pay for work they are not doing. Indeed, as technology improves and as ownership of new capital becomes more widespread, the income of our families would increase. This, in turn, would assure a growing buying power among the rank-

and-file citizenry, which is essential for the vitality and growth of our economy.[9]

The American people have not realistically adjusted to the changing productivity of capital and labor. Although a growing number of Americans have a form of capital and a source of future income from Social Security, pensions and retirement plans, the majority do not own enough capital to contribute significantly to their income. Indeed, many think only of labor as a source of income. They look to full employment as a panacea for the nation's economic problems. They even create situations that cause further concentration of capital ownership in their efforts to develop new jobs and increase workers' pay.

In many instances workers have claimed increased productivity (and demanded higher pay) when actually their contribution has decreased while the contribution of the machines they operate accounts for the increased productivity. This trend finds its ultimate term in featherbedding, the continuation of jobs that contribute nothing to the operation in question.

We are in agreement with the desire of workers to increase their income. Unless this occurs, they will not fully participate in the benefits of technological progress and their lack of buying power will cause a stagnation in the growth of markets for the products of our economy. However, we insist that most of this increased income should be derived from ownership of capital. Any other policy leads to a disorderly taking from the owners of capital the income that rightfully belongs to them.

It is ironic that millions of U.S. citizens suffer poverty in a nation of unparalleled affluence. This is due partly to the fact that a tiny minority of our citizens own and derive income from our productive property. This condition cuts off the poor from one of the two sources of income. In effect, we are asking the poor to climb the economic ladder with one leg.

There is a growing concern among leaders of the antipoverty effort in the United States to devise ways to help low-income people gain a stake in the productive property of the nation.

The Fathers of Vatican Council II remind us that personal liberty is inseparable from property: "Private property or some ownership of external goods confers on everyone a sphere wholly necessary for the autonomy of the person and the family, and it should be regarded as an extension of human freedom. Lastly, since it adds incentives for carrying on one's function and charge, it constitutes one of the conditions for civil liberties" (Constitution on the Church in the Modern World, par. 26). Ownership of property better enables an individual to protect his human rights. The people who do not own property—and they are a majority— lack this power. This is one source of their frustration and anger. The answer, however, is not to destroy the institution of private property, but to extend it. If property can confer dignity, material comfort and security upon the few, it can do the same for the many.

The modern popes have repeatedly stated that the right to own property is founded in human nature, and that it is conducive to the welfare of the individual, the family and society. At the same time, the popes have stressed the limitations of property rights and their social implications.

Back in 1891, Pope Leo XIII stated the Catholic position on property rights in his encyclical *On the Condition of Labor:* "For every man has by nature the right to possess property of his own" (par. 5). "That right of property, therefore, which has been proved to belong to individual persons must also belong to a man in his capacity of head of a family; nay, such a person must possess this right so much the more clearly in proportion as his position multiplies his duties" (par. 9). "Men always work harder and more readily when they work on that which is their own. . . . It is evident how much a spirit of willing labor would add to the produce of the earth and the wealth of the community" (par. 35). Thus, Pope Leo stated the import of private property for the individual, the family and society.

Membership in cooperatives such as those described in chapters 2 and 3 provide low-income people with modest income from stock (capital) they own. It also affords the co-op members some insight into the way in which capital is amassed and managed.

During recent years I have helped establish corporations that facilitate ownership of substantial capital by low-income people. First, the enterprise should be proven sound by thorough feasibility studies. For example, when the Human/Economic Appalachian Development (HEAD) Corporation started a sawmill in eastern Kentucky, they enlisted the services of the University of Kentucky to conduct a feasibility and marketing study. The conclusion of that study indicated that the proposed sawmill would be profitable.

Local people were invited to purchase small amounts of stock in the corporation, Mt. Top, Inc. The balance of the $850,000 capital invested in the sawmill was derived from loans, most of them "soft" loans made by foundations and federal agencies. As these loans are amortized from the profits of the sawmill, the value of the locally owned stock will increase. Eventually, all of these loans will be repaid and the value of the stock will be equal to the equity of the corporation. At this point, control over the company will pass to local stock owners. Thereafter, they will have a second income, derived from Mt. Top dividends.

During 1977, Mt. Top suffered financial problems due to low production and cash-flow shortages. To remedy these problems, the sawmill and a part of the site were released to other companies. I am convinced of the fundamental soundness of the Mt. Top plan and am confident that eventually Mt. Top will be completely owned by local stockholders.

Profit-sharing plans are still another way in which workers can derive significant income from capital. Such workers will be more concerned about their productivity, since their own income will be affected by the efficiency of the plant.

A strong argument can be made for tax laws that make ownership of capital more widespread. For example, a certain percentage of a person's income, which he chooses to convert into stock ownership, might be tax exempt. In the long run, this will result in more widespread ownership of capital, increased buying power by the poorer citizens and eventually an increment in tax revenues.

It is ironic that in the United States, where we so loudly defend capitalism, only about 5 percent of our citizens own significant amounts of income-earning property. To help the other 95 percent gain such ownership is a challenge deserving our attention.

5
Rural Communities Struggle for Survival

When I became the executive director of the National Catholic Rural Life Conference in June 1960, I was thrust into a tremendous struggle for survival that was unfolding in many communities in the United States. For many years, farms had been growing larger and the number of farm families in rural communities had decreased accordingly. This meant fewer people to trade on Main Street, fewer people in church on Sunday and a declining school population. Because economic opportunity in rural communities was meager, the brightest and most ambitious young people out-migrated to cities seeking jobs. Population in many rural communities had already been reduced to less than half of their peak numbers.

During the 1960s I became deeply involved in several hundred of these communities as they attempted to solve such problems through various self-help programs. One prominent feature of these efforts was unprecedented cooperation between agencies of federal and state governments and local leaders.

The Rural Areas Development Program (RAD), initiated by federal legislation in 1962, was a major feature of these joint efforts. The essential characteristics of RAD were the following. A group of local leaders formed a RAD committee, serving the county or in some instances two or more counties. After electing officers, their first practical action was to conduct a survey of their resources—usually with some help from the state college of agriculture. They then formed an Overall Economic Development Plan—projected fifteen or twenty years into the future.

According to RAD legislation, agencies of federal and state governments were required to give first priority to projects proposed by these local RAD committees. Ideally, then, the resources of the Farmers Home Administration, the Soil Conservation Service (SCS), the Extension Service, the Small Business Association, and so forth, were marshaled in a joint effort with local leaders toward meeting the felt needs of the community. RAD reflected self-help at its best. Whenever this plan was faithfully followed, it bore fruit.

During the first two years of this program over two thousand RAD committees were formed. During that period they completed 1,704 projects. Sixty-six thousand volunteer workers were actively engaged in RAD undertakings.

One of the most successful RAD programs occurred in Appanoose, Iowa. In 1960 Appanoose County had the lowest per capita income in the state of Iowa. The two chief industries, coal mining and agriculture, were badly depressed. Most of the mines were closed. Between 1920 and 1963, 95 percent of the jobs in the mining industry had been lost. The hilly farms of the county produced poor crops and sustained few cattle when left in pasture. Between 1920 and 1963 the net out-migration was 48.2 percent.

In 1961 local leaders formed a development committee. With the help of the staff at Iowa State University, they made a survey of resources and formed their Overall Economic Development Plan. Their first project was the building of the Golden Age Manor, which housed 100 senior citizens and provided employment for thirty-five persons. They nearly quadrupled the size of Centerville Junior College. Improvements at the college include a new electronics school. This means more faculty members, more jobs for maintenance and more young people to liven up the community.

During the winter of 1961, a series of meetings was held among farmers of the county with the help of the ASCS, SCS and the Extension Service. The farmers decided that they must move from open tillage of their hilly soil to a program of pasture improvement and cow herd expansion. Over two-thirds of them engaged in this project. ASCS provided cost-share grants for pasture improvement. Local bankers loaned money to farmers wishing to expand their cow herds. The result was a rapidly expanding and very profitable Feeder Cattle Program. This meant increased income for the farmers and more trade in Centerville, the county seat, and other towns of the county.

During the winter of 1961, a merchandising school was conducted with the help of the Extension Service. This resulted in a 12 percent increase in retail sales in the county during the ensuing year. Every business surrounding the city square in Centerville was refurbished.

The RAD committee approached locally owned factories in an effort to expand their operations. They discovered that the main requirement on the part of these companies was an assurance that the economy would not further deteriorate. This resulted in a quick doubling of the facilities of the Levine Company, a foundry, and the Fuller Manufacturing Company, which manufactures folding tables.

Meanwhile the Visking Division of Union Carbide Corporation was seeking a place to locate a new plant in which plastic food wrappers would be manufactured. They chose Centerville as their site, apparently because they liked the attitude of the people of that city — people who were looking forward instead of backward. This factory employs approximately four hundred persons. Soon thereafter, the McGraw-Edison Company established a large factory in Centerville for manufacturing electrical appliances, employing approximately three hundred thirty workers.

With a $200,000 grant from the Public Works Administration, the city of Centerville doubled its water facilities. Through a bond issue new streets were built; private investors built several new homes; St. Mary's Church, a frame structure, was replaced with a modern brick church; St. John's Hospital added significantly to its facilities.

The Army Corps of Engineers constructed a dam on the Chariton River near Rathbun in Appanoose County, thus creating a ten-thousand-acre lake. This opened up a significant recreational industry. Many families built summer homes on the shores of the lake. Several retail stores were founded to supply local people with boats, fishing equipment, and so forth.

Twice since leaving Iowa in 1971 I returned to Centerville and was pleased to note that in each instance new industrial developments were in evidence. This is proof that the revitalization of Appanoose County, begun in 1961, was established on proper foundations.

While RAD committees were strengthening the overall economies of many rural communities, there remained pockets of poverty within such communities. In an effort to serve such poverty groups, the Office of Economic Opportunity (OEO) attempted, during the mid-1960s, to extend its services to rural communities. The officers of the Rural Services Division of OEO soon found that they lacked effective contacts in the rural communities they proposed to serve. Realizing that I had such contacts, they enlisted my services to explain and initiate more than 100 antipoverty committees in rural communities throughout the nation. These antipoverty programs were directed by Community Action Committees (CAC), which observed most of the self-help principles described in Chapter 1. CACs analyzed the needs of low-income people of the area and proposed steps to meet such needs. In many instances there was not yet in existence a program providing the services required. For example, Head Start programs were initiated in many communities to provide essential training for preschool children of low-income families. Job Corps camps were established in strategic places throughout the nation to prepare for unemployment young adults who lacked the most fundamental skills. Special services such as nutrition, health and recreation were also provided for the senior citizens of the area.[10]

Many rural antipoverty programs were only modestly successful. As indicated above, the task of forming CACs in rural areas was more difficult than in cities. By the time these rural committees were formed, a significant curtailment of OEO funds had already occurred. Moreover, the rural poor are more scattered and less effectively organized than the urban poor. It was also very difficult to identify leadership among the rural poor. Nevertheless, CACs were and remain a significant force for self-determination among the poor of rural America.

The outstanding—and most controversial—characteristic of CACs is their providing low-income people with a vehicle for self-determination. In many communities the power structure resisted the establishing of CACs for this reason. Much of the congressional opposition to the OEO was rooted in this same conflict. Hence, CACs have had a stormy existence. Often they had to function on emergency funds. Yet, most of them have survived. This is a witness to the deep-rooted desire on the part of disadvantaged people for some means of guiding their own economic destinies.

6
Field Workers Unionize

As indicated in the Introduction, for nearly a century unions have been the chief means through which craftsmen and industrial workers exercise their right to self-determination. This basic right was denied American farm workers until a decade ago when Cesar Chavez and his colleagues appeared on the scene in the rich agricultural valleys of California.[11]

In 1932 the Wagner Act was adopted by Congress protecting the right of industrial workers to organize and bargain collectively. Farm workers were excluded from its provisions. Congress feared that the opposition of the powerful farm bloc would have caused the defeat of the Wagner Act if farm workers had been included in its provisions. This exclusion continues to this day in federal farm legislation.

The achievement of Cesar Chavez and his supporters is all the more amazing when we note that he has organized some of the most vulnerable and insecure of all workers, those who harvest fruits and vegetables. This is seasonal work. Most pickers migrate as the crops mature. Prior to Chavez, efforts to organize these workers had failed. The opposition by growers to unionization was so ruthless and the field workers were so vulnerable that it was presumed back in 1960 that unionization was for them indeed "the impossible dream."

Books such as Steinbeck's *Grapes of Wrath* during the 1930s and Edward R. Murrow's television documentary *Harvest of Shame* during 1960 chronicle the tragic exploitation experienced by these most disadvantaged of American workers.

Much has been written about Chavez and the Farm Workers Union. I shall report the main events of this saga as I viewed it in my capacity as executive director of the National Catholic Rural Life Conference (NCRLC) from 1960 to 1971, as bishop of a diocese with a large farm population and as a member of the American Bishops' Committee on Farm Labor from 1972 to date.

Cesar Chavez was born on March 31, 1927, the second son of Librado and Juana Chavez. As a child Cesar shared with his family the hardships of migrant workers and the humiliations of camp life. His family migrated each year from the Imperial to the Sacramento Valleys.

Cesar served in the South Pacific during World War II. At the conclusion of the war he returned to Delano, California, where he resumed his role as a field worker.

A significant turning point in Chavez's life occurred in 1958 when he met and became a co-worker with Father Donald McDonald, then the Rural Life Director of the San Francisco Archdiocese. From Father McDonald Cesar learned well the Church's social teachings as presented in the great encyclicals of the modern popes. This orientation toward social justice has been apparent in the speeches, writings and actions of Chavez from that date to this. Perhaps this contact with Father McDonald further explains the strong commitment of Chavez to nonviolence.

When I first visited California in the fall of 1960, Chavez was employed by the Community Service Organization (CSO), founded by Fred Ross, Sr., during the 1940s to foster self-help for Mexican Americans in urban areas. One of the purposes of my visit to California was to give some guidance in the use of a $10,000 grant that NCRLC was making at that time to CSO. It was on that occasion that I first met Dolores Huerte, who has been a close associate of Chavez from the late fifties until the present time. At that time Chavez was trying to interest the workers near Oxnard, California, in unionization.

Eventually, in 1962, he resigned from CSO because he found the urban-minded board of directors of the organization disinterested in agricultural workers and an obstacle to his chief concern, namely, to help these workers form a union. At about the same time, I had two experiences in California that dramatized the need for unionization among farm workers. With a great deal of planning and labor, I led an effort to conduct a massive adult education program on Christian social principles in all of the dioceses of that state. The *Central Catholic Register* had printed the informational materials and discussion outlines we had prepared for this purpose. Sufficient numbers were printed to put one into practically every Catholic home in the state. It soon became apparent that a very large proportion of the Catholic people of California was simply not interested in a study of this sort.

This attitude was brought home to me forcefully in the fall of 1962 when Bishop Hugh Donohoe, then Bishop of Stockton, and I met in Stockton with a very influential group of growers. I made a brief exposition of the Christian principles that I felt should regulate the relationships between growers and workers. A spokesman for the growers interrupted and advised Bishop Donohoe and me that they had the *power* to run farm labor relations as they were at that time. If we ever had the *power* to force them to do otherwise, we should inform them. The meeting broke up.

This is precisely the kind of experience that prompted Chavez and others to conclude that the only way in which workers' rights would be respected would be a situation in which they had the power to demand those rights. All appeals to conscience had, up to that time, failed. Unionization seemed, and probably truly is, the only available means through which workers can gain the power to protect their fundamental rights.

At that time in California a significant obstacle to unionization was the importation of 300,000 "braceros," each year. These braceros were brought from Mexico without families to work in the fields for a specified number of weeks and then were returned to their homeland. Any effort at unionization would be extremely difficult so long as the farmers had this kind of easily manipulated labor supply at their disposal. We in the NCRLC had fought the bracero program vigorously for many years. Eventually the program was ended in December 1963.

Meanwhile Cesar Chavez was forming that which he called the National Farm Workers Association (NFWA). By September 30, 1962, he claimed between 250 and 300 family members. Between 1962 and 1965 NFWA became involved in a few short-lived strikes in the vegetable and fruit ranches of California. Meanwhile, in 1957 Filipino farm workers formed the Agricultural Workers Organizing Committee (AWOC) and affiliated with AFL-CIO.

A significant new era in California agriculture began in September 1965 when NFWA joined AWOC in a grape strike. This struggle lasted five years. One of the major tactics used by the NFWA was the secondary boycott. Many thousands of sympathizers in cities and towns throughout the nation agreed to boycott grapes until a settlement of the strike had been reached.

The following is a brief chronicle of events between 1966 and 1973:

Aug. 1966	AWOC and NFWA merge to form the United Farm Workers Organizing Committee (UFWOC), AFL-CIO.
1966– 1967	UFWOC wins elections and signs contracts with Christian Brothers, Gallo, Almaden, Italian Swiss Colony and Paul Masson wineries.
Apr.– July 1970	The American Bishops' Committee on Farm Workers, headed by the late Bishop Joseph Donnelly, are invited to act as conciliators in the long grape strike. Monsignor George Higgins of the U.S. Catholic Conference provides valuable staff assistance to the committee. Finally, on July 29, 1970, twenty-six grape growers sign an agreement with UFWOC.
July 23, 1970	With grape strike and boycott coming to end, UFWOC sends telegrams asking for union recognition from lettuce growers in Salinas, Santa Maria and Imperial Valleys. Salinas growers meet and decide to "feel

out the Teamsters" about a contract for field workers (this fact testified to in court by Cal Watkins of United Fruit on Sept. 1, 1970).

Summer 1970
UFWOC repeatedly requests elections at lettuce farms. Teamsters and UFWOC announce new jurisdictional agreement.

Aug. 11, 1970
Teamsters agree to withdraw from lettuce contracts. Catholic Bishops' Committee witnesses agreement. Growers refuse to sign with UFWOC.

Aug. 24, 1970
Seven thousand lettuce workers strike growers with Teamster sweetheart contracts and ask for representational elections. The *Los Angeles Times* calls it the largest farm labor strike in U.S. history.

March 26, 1971
Teamsters and UFWOC sign three-year agreement countersigned by Meany of the AFL-CIO and Fitzsimmons of the Teamsters.

Feb. 1972
AFL-CIO grants UFWOC an independent charter. New name: United Farm Workers (UFW).

April 16, 1973
Majority of Coachella Valley table grape growers refuse to renew contracts with UFW, signing instead with the Teamsters. Strike and renewed grape boycott begin.

Summer 1973
San Joaquin Valley Growers also sign contracts with Teamsters. On strike lines, mass arrests of farm workers and supporters are made, including many religious supporters.

Oct. 1973   Boycott continues worldwide against non-UFW table grapes and head lettuce and Gallo Wines. (Gallo had signed a sweetheart contract with the Teamsters at the same time as many of the grape growers after six years under UFW contract.)

In November 1973 the National Conference of Catholic Bishops (NCCB) unanimously adopted the following resolution: "The NCCB endorses and supports the UFW's consumer boycott of table grapes and head lettuce until such time as free, secret ballot elections are held." This endorsement greatly strengthened Chavez's efforts to bring about bona fide bargaining by the growers.

On June 5, 1975, the state of California enacted an Agriculture Labor Relations Act that designated the manner in which labor contracts and other labor relations in California agriculture should be conducted.

This legislation was highly acclaimed by most Americans at that time. Bishop Roger Mahoney, who had served for some years as the secretary of the American Bishops' Farm Labor Committee, was appointed the first chairman of the California Agriculture Labor Relations Board. That board then made a monumental effort to supervise elections in the disputed lettuce and other fields of California, to let the workers decide whether they wished a union and, if so, whether they preferred UFW or the Teamsters. The number of elections to be supervised, the mobility of many of the workers and the extent of conflict among the parties concerned made this an extremely difficult task.

Early in 1976 the California Agriculture Labor Relations Board ran out of money. Opponents of UFW proceeded to pressure the California legislature to severely undercut the main features of this labor act as a price that would be exacted for authorizing emergency funds for the board. Since a two-thirds majority was required for such emergency funding, these growers and their associates felt they had the upper hand. This tactic boomeranged. Most observers in California and throughout the nation vociferously objected to this kind of "blackmail." Eventually the legislature provided the necessary funds without substantial changes in the state agricultural law.

Meanwhile the Teamsters were faring very badly in the above-mentioned election. They simply had very little support from the rank-and-file field workers. After many false starts, on March 10, 1977, UFW and the International Brotherhood of Teamsters signed a jurisdictional pact according to which UFW would attempt to organize only workers employed in circumstances described in the California Agriculture Labor Relations Act and the Teamsters would organize only those workers covered by the National Labor Relations Act. This represented a victory for Chavez and his associates.

It is still too early in this process fully to evaluate the significance of Chavez's efforts. It can be safely said that there is now a very great probability that unions truly representative of the rank-and-file field workers will continue to grow not only in California but in all regions where there are significant numbers of fruit and vegetable workers.

Seldom in the history of our nation has any group of Americans struggled against such monumental odds and suffered so valiantly for so long a period for a cause. This represents a dimension of self-help that deserves careful attention. It is apparent that, if a group of low-income people truly determine to work together and to help themselves, no coalition of economic, political and other forces is able to withstand them. The possibility of gaining adequate income, decent living conditions and a truly human role in society is now, for the first time, opening up to our agricultural workers, particularly those who harvest our fruit and vegetable crops.

7
American Indians
Seek Self-Determination

The self-determination now sought by American Indians is significantly broader in scope than that sought by other citizens. Not only are the Indians seeking economic development and social justice; they are struggling to preserve their culture and social institutions, which are sharply in contrast with those of the majority of Americans. In America today there are 250 Indian tribes and bands speaking 200 languages. There is a long and sad history of conflict and exploitation of Indians by white men in this nation.[12] Indians now represent less than 1 percent of our population. The majority live on reservations where they can pursue to a certain degree their tribal traditions, but where economic and social opportunities are usually extremely limited. Many Indian youths have migrated to cities seeking educational and employment opportunities. They have experienced severe pressure as they try to reconcile their basic inclination toward tribal living with the extremely individualistic living that prevails in the typical American city.

In 1976 the Catholic bishops of Minnesota published a statement entitled "A New Beginning," followed by six months of intense dialogue between representatives of the dioceses and of the Indian tribes of the state. Several substantial steps have been taken to improve the relationship between the Indians and the Church in Minnesota.

During May 1977 the American bishops issued a somewhat similar statement on the Church's relationship with the American Indian. The bishops strongly affirmed the right of Indians to preserve their social and cultural traditions. They called upon all agencies of the Church to include Indians more extensively in planning activities that affect them.

For many years Catholic agencies such as Catholic Charities, Catholic Mission among the Colored People and Indians and the Bureau of Catholic Indian Missions have served needs of Indians. More recently, the Campaign for Human Development (CHD) has directed substantial funds to support self-help projects on Indian reservations and among other Indian groups. The CHD represents a significant step in the direction that the Indians themselves earnestly desire.

American Indians need the help of other citizens in their struggle to obtain essential political rights. Since they are such a tiny minority, there is a tendency for government to be unresponsive to their rights and demands. Particularly urgent are treaty and statute issues that are pending in Congress and in several state legislatures. Moreover, if Indians are to overcome their significant economic disadvantages, more generous technical assistance must be extended to them.

In my capacity as executive director of the National Catholic Rural Life Conference, I assisted during the 1960s in several self-help programs in which Indians were engaged. The following is a brief description of three of the most significant of these programs.

The Southwest Indian Foundation was established

by the Franciscan Fathers at Gallup, New Mexico, in 1968. Since that time $2,697,857.78 worth of assistance has been supplied by the foundation to various self-help projects in which the Navajo Indians of the area have engaged. For example, one of the first enterprises established by the Navajo Indians was a factory that manufactures prefabricated houses. This not only provides employment to many of the local Indians; it also makes available to them quality housing at a reasonable price.

During 1969 the Southwest Indian Foundation provided timely financial assistance to a home-improvement project at the Indian village at Church Rock, New Mexico. During one eight-week period, forty-seven apartments were painted inside and given new roofs or new floors and equipped with new windows and doors. The work was done by the people of the village. The Southwest Indian Foundation provided funds to purchase the necessary equipment and building materials.

Many of the Navajo Indians live in "hogans," which are very uncomfortable shacks made of logs and dirt. The Southwest Indian Foundation has assisted many families of the area as they put windows and new roofs on their hogans and added new rooms to them. The results are very modest dwellings but they are vastly more comfortable and conducive to health than the original hogans were.

During 1970, the Southwest Indian Foundation helped finance the building of a preschool at the Navajo Reservation near Many Farms, Arizona. The initiative for starting the school came from the Indians of the Red Rock Chapter of the reservation who also provided the labor. The Southwest Indian Foundation contributed funds for the roof of the building.

Following the policy of the Southwest Indian

Foundation to respond to the felt needs of the people, it has engaged in building more than fifty bridges over dry river beds, called arroyos, in the area. When the rains come, these arroyos become raging streams, isolating families from work, school and medical services. In each instance the foundation provided most of the money needed for materials; the people of the area provided the labor.

Life on the Navajo Reservation is grim by American standards. The timely financial assistance provided by the Southwest Indian Foundation has enabled the Navajo Indians to significantly improve their living conditions. Most importantly, it has been done in a manner in which the tribe itself has maintained initiative and control and significantly strengthened its self-esteem.

During the middle 1960s, the Chippewa Indians at Turtle Mountain Reservation, North Dakota, formed a Community Action Committee. This committee continues to function, providing Head Start training for preschoolers; also, for the aged Indians of the reservation, a seventy-two unit retirement center has been constructed. One of the major industries started in the early 1960s at the reservation is the William Langer Jewel Bearing Company. Presently employed at that factory are 150 local Indians who have extremely great patience and skill in manufacturing tiny jewel bearings for delicate instruments. The federal Department of Housing and Urban Development has financed hundreds of new homes for the Indians of this reservation. In the meanwhile an increasing number of Indians are entering into small retail and service enterprises. Many of them have acquired skills as electricians, plumbers, television repairmen, and so forth, at the United Tribes Training Center in Bismark.

On April 30, 1961, the Menominee Reservation west of Green Bay, Wisconsin, was terminated and the residents of the area became members of a new Menominee County. From the outset this was an extremely controversial move by our federal government—so much so that during 1973 President Nixon signed a Restoration Act making Menominee County a reservation once more. The following are some of the issues at stake.

The Menominees were permitted to vote for or against termination, but there is evidence that they lacked clear information regarding the choices open to them. Some of them were under the impression that termination would occur regardless of their vote. They were also led to believe that failure to approve termination would cause them to lose a substantial sum of money owed them by the government as a consequence of a court suit.

In my estimation, termination of a reservation is a critical step. It should never be taken with incomplete information regarding alternatives and never under duress.

Menominee County has a population of approximately three thousand, almost all of whom are Indians. It is extremely difficult to maintain the services of a county government with so small a population. In the future, Indians should be incorporated into counties only where there is a population of eight to twelve thousand or more. Many of the fiscal problems of Menominee County are due to the small population, not to the residents' failure to govern themselves wisely.

During the transition period, from 1961 to 1973, the federal government and the state of Wisconsin made commendable efforts to assist the Menominees in functions of county government such as schools and welfare programs. This has prevented some of the serious in-adequacies that would have otherwise occurred in these institutions and programs.

Even after termination, the Menominees were not prepared for private ownership of property in our sense of the term. They chose to create a corporation, Menominee Enterprises, Inc., which owns most of the property and conducts most of the enterprises in the county. Stock in the corporation was issued to citizens of the county. However, the stock of the minors and incompetents of the county was administered as a trust by a local bank.

Constantly plagued with financial problems, Menominee County was forced eventually to sell a section of the county (8,000 acres) to private entrepreneurs who developed a resort area called Legend Lake. Harvesting timber from the forest of the county remains one of the chief sources of income.

The process of restoration has continued from 1973 to date. In 1975 the restoration of the reservation was made official, and Menominee Tribal Enterprises was formed to take charge of most projects of the reservation. In 1976 the tribe was given jurisdiction over certain civil and criminal matters and a constitution and by-laws were adopted. Presently efforts are being made to elect a tribal legislature.

Rightly planned and freely chosen, termination of a reservation might afford Indians a release from the white man's paternalism and new opportunities for self-government. However, if this road is taken in other reservations, the mistakes made in the Menominee County termination should be carefully avoided.

The problems of American Indians remain one of the most distressing issues confronting us today. It is not yet clear how these problems may be resolved. However, I am convinced that self-help and self-determination of the sort described above represent at least a significant part of such solutions.

8
Campaign for Human Development

The preceding chapters have focused on grass-roots organizations engaged in self-help projects. The Campaign for Human Development (CHD) has as one of its major objectives providing financial support to such projects. The second objective is to educate the American public about the extent of poverty here, its causes, its effects and its remedies. Doubtless, the extent to which this second objective is accomplished will greatly affect the response of the American people to the annual appeal for contributions to support self-help projects.

This annual collection is taken up in Catholic parishes of the nation at Thanksgiving time. Fifty-four million dollars have been contributed since CHD was inaugurated in 1970. Twenty-five percent of the funds collected is used for self-help projects in the local dioceses; the remaining 75 percent is distributed through the National Campaign Office in Washington, D.C. Approximately $37 million have been forwarded to this office, where distribution has been made to fund 1,120 projects.

This national distribution is controlled by a forty-member board with practical experience in problems of poverty. It is representative of black, white, Indian, Oriental and Spanish-speaking groups from throughout the nation. Committee members recommend to the Bishops' Committee specific projects for funding and provide counsel to campaign staff in developing allocation norms and educational and promotional priorities concerning poverty and human development.

To receive CHD funds, a project must satisfy the following criteria:

1. Most of those benefiting from a project must be from low-income groups.

2. The poor must have the dominant voice in any self-help project.

3. Funding will not be considered for projects that can be adequately funded by monies known to be available from the private or public sector.

4. The project activity for which funding is requested must conform to the moral teaching of the Church.

High priority is given to projects with the following qualifications:

1. Promising, innovative projects that demonstrate a change from traditional approaches to poverty;

2. Projects that directly benefit a large number of people rather than a few individuals;

3. Projects that generate cooperation among and within diverse groups.

National campaign projects fall into the following categories: social development, economic development, health, communications, legal aid, housing, education and transportation. The national campaign staff keeps in close contact with the CHD director and the bishop of the diocese from which a grant is sought. In the follow-up, careful evaluation is made of the effectiveness with which the grant monies have been used.

During the months in which CHD was being planned and launched, I was involved by reason of my position in the National Catholic Rural Life Conference, which was then a part of the Social Action Department of the U.S. Catholic Conference. During those deliberations, I injected my strong convictions about the import of true self-help policies on the part of any organization receiving CHD funds. During the first year of fund distribution, I provided staff evaluation of all rural development projects submitted for funding. Now, as the bishop of Peoria, I vigorously promote both the educational and the funding dimensions of CHD. The diocese of Peoria adds $35,000 to the 25 percent of the CHD collection that is retained in our diocese. Our diocesan Social Action Committee then distributes these funds, usually amounting to about $70,000 per year, to worthy self-help projects in or about the diocese.

Unquestionably, the more than $54 million contributed by American Catholics during the past six years represent a substantial boost to self-help.

Equally significant is the educational component of CHD. This is a twelve-month-a-year campaign to sensitize Americans to the extent and tragedy of poverty, to help effect attitudinal changes toward the poor and to stimulate programs to eradicate poverty. The staff at the CHD national office and Diocesan Educational Coordinators in 160 dioceses spearhead this component of the campaign. The national educational staff has participated in over one hundred workshops and seminars on this topic. They also make available to schools and CCD classes literature and audiovisual tools. Numerous television and radio spot announcements and clips are supplied to bring poverty issues to the attention of the general public. Finally, the projects funded represent a significant educational effort. This includes much listening to low-income people and testing through them various antipoverty proposals.

Thus, the educational component of CHD is a significant service to Americans in general. There are few afflictions so incongruous as ignorance or indifference toward the poverty of our fellowmen.

9
Self-Help in U.S. Cities

The self-help programs described in the preceding chapters are by and for rural people. This concentration on rural self-help is partly due to the fact that I am reporting chiefly on programs in which I have been involved. Those programs have been largely in rural communities.

Let us now direct our attention to self-help projects in which urban low-income people have engaged. Some of the circumstances prevailing in inner cities militate against the sort of self-help programs described in chapter 1. Urban life, particularly in the slums, tends to isolate individuals from their neighbors and reduce neighborhood cooperation. Furthermore, the needs of our inner cities are so many and so deep rooted that most private organizations find it extremely difficult to cope with them.

However, during recent years a significant number of self-help programs have emerged in American cities. The following is a description of some of those projects drawn primarily from the files of the Campaign for Human Development (CHD), which has evaluated and supported many urban self-help projects during the past six years. Self-help in cities differs in several significant ways from rural self-help. First, a significant objective of the former is an effort to channel more governmental assistance to the urban poor. This involves political action. Consider, for example, Communities Organized for Major Service (COPS) in San Antonio's west-south-side barrios, where approximately 76,500 Mexican Americans live. Begun in 1973, COPS has won for their constituents over $55 million in government grants for capital improvements in Mexican American neighborhoods. Back in 1974, COPS pressured city hall for a $45 million bond issue to deal with serious drainage problems in their part of the city. Voters passed it overwhelmingly. When San Antonio received $16 million from the federal government under the Community Development Act (CDA), COPS drew up an alternate budget for the use of the grant. Thus, COPS caused the redirection of $12.3 million of the $16 million for use in neighborhood projects.

COPS has joined with groups in other parts of the city to achieve mutual goals. This coalition halted the building of a shopping center over the Aquifer, San Antonio's only water supply.

COPS pressures financial institutions as well as governmental bodies. In an effort to counter "redlining" practices by local financial institutions, COPS has organized a "greenlining" campaign, whereby local churches, community organizations, small businessmen and concerned citizens pleged to withdraw their funds from institutions unresponsive to the financial needs of barrios and deposit them in banks and savings and loan companies willing to invest in these neighborhoods.

Self-help as practiced by COPS differs in a significant way from that practiced by Southern Consumers Cooperative in Louisiana or by the cooperatives organized by the poor of Appalachia. The latter often seek assistance from governmental agencies to supplement their own monies and labors. COPS makes the redistribution of tax money its major objective. COPS is primarily political; most rural self-help programs are not.

In light of the monumental problems of urban slums and the large sums being expended by local, state and federal governments for urban renewal, grass-roots political action is certainly indicated.

We might inquire about the impact these two approaches to self-help have on the participants' dignity and self-esteem. A successful exercise of political power by a previously powerless group of impoverished peoples is exhilarating. Father Albert Benevides, a pastor on San Antonio's west side and an active COPS participant, states that the Mexican American people of his neighborhood "have been touched and transformed dramatically. They will never be the same." Maria Valenzuela, who has lived in Immaculate Conception Parish, San Antonio, for twenty-five years, states: "COPS is something to be proud of. We know for a fact that COPS is getting to the places of most need. We used to feel sorry for ourselves. Now we are getting out of this hole we were in for so many, many years." Referring to governmental officials, Maria declares: "They think because we're poor, we're ignorant. Well we're not. We are just poor. That's why we have COPS."

Throughout its often controversial history, COPS has received the blessing of Bishop Patricio Flores, the first Mexican American bishop, and strong encouragement and financial support from Archbishop Francis Furey of San Antonio. In 1975 CHD provided COPS a $45,000 grant.

The most significant COPS victory has not been their millions of dollars for capital investment, but rather their effect on the way political decisions are made. Mrs. Valenzuela puts it: "It's good to know little people can stand up together and be heard." Most of us would agree that the mentality of a Mrs. Valenzuela is preferable to that of a hopeless and embittered slum dweller. On the other hand, her self-help experience differs substantially from that of Nancy Cole, who helped the people of Eastern Kentucky make themselves significantly less dependent upon governmental grants and handouts by producing and selling cooperatively high-quality handicrafts. The feeling of power and self-determination reflected in Mrs. Valenzuela's remarks are closely akin to those experienced by members of the United Farm Workers as they gained the power to bargain collectively for their rights. In other words, Nancy Cole and Maria Valenzuela reflect two related but significantly different components of self-help. The former is a gain of independence from outside help; the latter is a gain of more control over outside help.

The following are additional illustrations of urban self-help with a strong emphasis on political action. The Milwaukee Alliance of Concerned Citizens (MACC) is a coalition of three community organizations that merged to mobilize "neighborhood power" on a city-wide scale. Among their targets are unfair taxation, scarce and low-grade housing, unpaved streets and lack of job-training opportunities. Among MACC's accomplishments is an end to "redlining" for all of Wisconsin. One of the organizations that merged with MACC was the Westside Action Coalition. In order to stop the deterioration of the Westside neighborhood, this organization helped persuade the Wisconsin State Legislature to outlaw redlining, the practice whereby lending institutions refuse to make home construction and home improvement loans to individuals in a specific geographic area. Low- and moderate-income people all over Wisconsin will benefit from the measure, and in the case of Westside, over $1 million in mortgage money has now returned to the neighborhood. CHD has funded the city-wide project for $25,000.

Since inadequate housing is a major curse in urban slums, many urban self-help programs address this problem. For example, Poor People Pulling Together (PPPT) was organized with a $15,000 CHD grant in 1972 in Las Vegas, Nevada. It is an organization of black urban dwellers, mostly residents of low-income housing projects.

PPPT has successfully influenced the local housing authority to adopt and implement a plan insuring that no tenant in public housing may be charged in excess of one quarter of his or her income. A food stamp program was initiated in 1972, also by PPPT. In 1973 and 1974, with the total aid of $60,000 in CHD funds, PPPT convinced the Department of Housing and Urban Development to prod the local housing authority to undertake restoration of run-down housing units. Other accomplishments include exposure of mismanagement of a federal housing construction program, appointment of a PPPT representative to a City of Las Vegas Task Force on housing issues, a $175,000 Community Development Act grant to establish a Home Owners Management Educational Center, and a gift of a parcel of land for development as a community center and as a resource of sustaining income.

When the residents of San Francisco's Chinatown organized "Chinese for Affirmative Action" (CAA) in 1969, they set as their major goals overcoming their political powerlessness and communicating their needs through existing political and social channels. A major goal is the full implementation of the 1975 bilingual amendments to the Voting Rights Act, the federal law paving the way for tens of thousands of non-English-speaking citizens to register and vote. With a Latino group, CAA brought suit against the city and county of San Francisco to set up trilingual registration centers, media messages and election signs and materials in compliance with the law.

CAA has also been successful in strengthening Chinese American representation on influential government boards and commissions. Members of the Chinese community now sit on five city commissions, including social services, human rights and manpower planning, and on six state boards, including fair employment practices, employment services, manpower development and bilingual voting.

CHD funds have also been instrumental in helping CAA develop programs for job placement and media access. CAA maintains a skills bank for more than one thousand persons; it has placed more than one hundred Chinese Americans in full-time employment and has assisted more than seventy in combating employment discrimination.

Legal services are a need closely akin to the political action described above. Advocates for Basic Legal Equality (ABLE) was organized in Toledo, Ohio, to win law reform and legal services for low-income citizens. ABLE has successfully reduced employment discrimination in the police and fire departments of Toledo, as well as in the Sheet Metal Workers Union. ABLE has also established the right to treatment for all patients in Ohio's mental institutions, is working for open-housing legislation and for bilingual, bicultural programs in public schools and is currently involved with public utility rate hikes and urban renewal.

Legal Services for Hungry Americans (FRAC) of New York City works in conjunction with other national and local poor peoples' groups as the nation's only poor peoples' legal and research center dealing with the fight against hunger in America. FRAC's principal objective is to work for basic changes in the governmental institutions that administer food assistance programs so that poor peoples' full legal rights to adequate nutrition will be guaranteed. FRAC brought suit against the U.S. Department of Agriculture, an action that resulted in the release of $278 million from the funds appropriated by Congress for the food stamp program for FY 1973. If it had not been for FRAC, those funds would have been returned to the U.S. Treasury.

Although political action is a major objective of urban self-help organizations, some do pursue self-help goals similar to those described in chapter 1. Such an organization is Brothers Redevelopment, Inc. (BRI) of Denver, Colorado. BRI offers planning and technical assistance free of charge to homeowners who cannot afford commercial home repair. The self-help concept is a requirement in this housing program. Property owners buy materials and necessary permits and work with volunteers to provide the manual labor. Free counsel on available loans and governmental assistance programs is offered by BRI. BRI has repaired more than 125 homes. CHD has contributed $110,000 to BRI, and many other religious denominations have also contributed to this project. The state of Colorado, recognizing the worth of this self-help program, extended to it a $50,000 grant in 1974.

Solidaridad Humana of New York City is a Hispanic educational program, which expanded through successive CHD grants in 1973 and 1974 ($42,000 total) from an apartment-based volunteer staff to an effort with a full-time teacher/coordinator and a part-time staff of fourteen. Originally designed to prepare young workers to take the high school equivalency exams in Spanish, the project now includes the arrangement of post-high school placements at the college level, as well as tutorial assistance. Lehman College in New York has also designated a bilingual college-level program in association with Solidaridad Humana. More than one hundred people have successfully completed the equivalency exam, of whom fifty are now college students.

United Indians of All Tribes Foundation (UIATF) is a community organization working to develop self-determination for all Native Americans in the Seattle area. Since 1973 the foundation has demonstrated the unique potential of merging arts, economic development and education to combat the poverty that has often characterized Indians' existence in cities. This existence was plagued for many years by substandard housing, poor education opportunities, high unemployment rates, poor health and government agency neglect. Cut off from a rich heritage and isolated from the non-Indian community, many felt helpless to break the cycle of powerlessness or to communicate their needs. Through UIATF, Native Americans of the Seattle area are attempting to provide a voice for their concerns. Through a $50,000 CHD grant, UIATF established a National Indian Communications Center. Through the communications center, Native Americans are conveying their concerns among Indian groups and to larger institutions affecting their lives.

A second CHD-funded project, Native American Arts and Crafts, provides a much-needed marketing service for Native American products. Many articles of high artistic value were being sold on a need-cash basis. Indian craftsmen were exploited by middlemen. Now the UIATF business has begun to reverse this pattern by establishing retail and wholesale outlets.

This brief survey of urban self-help programs reflects typical responses of urban low-income people of various races to the massive problems with which they are faced. Although these projects are too few in number and too small in scope to substantially change urban poverty at this time, they point to solutions that might be embraced more extensively in the future.

10
International Voluntary Services

No other organization emphasizes the principles of self-help listed in chapter 1 so uncompromisingly as does the International Voluntary Services (IVS). Volunteers of this organization have served with great dedication in some of the poorest and most troubled Third World nations.

IVS was founded in 1953 by fourteen men drawn from religious, educational and governmental organizations of the United States. They wished to introduce a new factor, close contact with village people, into the overseas programs of this nation. In its first two decades of operation, IVS worked closely with the U.S. government and the governments of Third World nations. Most of its financial support was derived from contracts negotiated with the U.S. Agency for International Development (USAID), stipulating person-to-person services that IVS volunteers would perform. In recent years, however, IVS has broadened its funding base to include more private organizations, such as foundations and church groups. More funds are also derived from private host institutions and governments in countries where IVS works.

Leaders of IVS throughout its twenty-four-year

history have maintained that volunteers could establish a special rapport with Third World people in sharing their skills with them, so that those skills could then be adapted for local use. Back in 1953 this seemed a bizarre suggestion. Critics described it as sending youngsters to do an adult's job.

The guiding principles of IVS are as follows:

1. *Program Focus* — IVS concentrates on recruiting volunteer technicians for projects that most directly help poorer rural people improve their lives and living conditions by their own efforts. IVS volunteers currently work in some of the world's poorest nations, and priority is given to such countries in developing new programs.

2. *Role of Volunteers* — The main role of the IVS technician is to help the host agency make a more effective contribution to local development. Usually this means IVS volunteers work at the village level, sharing their technical knowledge and experience with local people. They also seek to work themselves out of their jobs, by transferring their skills to counterpart workers who can take over the volunteers' functions. In the field, IVS volunteers work for the host agencies to which they are assigned, not IVS.

3. *Recruitment* — IVS volunteers are recruited only in response to specific requests from host governments and institutions. As a small, specialist agency, IVS matches skills to needs in supplying volunteers in four main skill areas allied to rural development. These are: agriculture, public health, small business/cooperative development and engineering. So the volunteers, who range in age from twenty-five to sixty-seven, include agronomists, horticulturalists, soil scientists, nurses, midwives, nutritionists, village technology specialists, civil, mechanical and water

engineers, and community development specialists.

4. *The International Dimension* — IVS is an international organization, and it is international in its volunteers, staff, recruitment and fund raising. IVS technicians come from all over the world through an international recruitment network covering Africa, Asia, Latin America, Europe and North America. This global network gives IVS greater opportunity to find the right candidate to fill a particular position and so respond better to local needs and priorities in developing countries. For, in the agency's experience, no one country has available specialists in the full range of skills most relevant to development. In September 1977, nearly 40 percent of IVS volunteers and field staff were from countries outside North America, including France, the Netherlands, Sweden, United Kingdom, the Philippines, Taiwan, Sri Lanka, Ecuador, Columbia and Haiti. In keeping with its policy of genuinely reflecting the "international" in its title, IVS hopes to increase the number of non-North Americans in the field to more than half by 1979. To achieve this, IVS has opened an office in Europe and is strengthening its worldwide recruitment network.

5. *Funding* — IVS funds come from many different sources, including private donors such as foundations and church groups. USAID provides about half the financial support. Host governments and institutions also make a contribution, usually sharing the costs of placing and maintaining volunteers in the field. IVS believes diversity and flexibility in funding is crucial to the organization's independence. To broaden its financial base, it is looking to different sources, with a priority on securing funds outside the United States and, in particular, from Europe.

From 1960 to 1970 I served as a member of the IVS

Board of Directors and as president of that board from 1965 to 1968. My involvement in the organization's efforts was very deep. During my period as president, I helped in the orientation of all the volunteers and made three around-the-world trips—in 1966, 1968 and 1969—to visit volunteers serving in Vietnam, Laos and Morocco.

The following list of places where IVS has served demonstrates the fact that IVSers go to some of the most troubled and impoverished nations of the Third World:

1955–1957 Iraq and Syria
1955 United Arab Republic and Jordan
1956–1958 Nepal and Sabah
1956–1975 Laos
1957–1959 Cambodia
1957–1971 Vietnam
1959–1963 Liberia and Ghana
1963–1967; 1968–1977 Algeria
1970–1972 Morocco
1971–1973 Libya and Zaire
1971–1977 Indonesia
1971–1977 Yemen
1973–1977 Bangladesh and Sudan
1973–1975 Madagascar
1974–1977 Ecuador, Honduras, Papua New Guinea
1975–1977 Botswana and Mauritania
1977 Bolivia

During the past fifteen years, the number of IVS volunteers serving overseas has ranged from seventy to about two hundred fifty. The largest teams were those serving in Vietnam and Laos during the mid-1960s.

In each IVS contract with the U.S. government or a foreign government or private agency, one or more specific services were stipulated. Most of these services related to agriculture, education or community development. However, with the recent change in IVS program direction, the focus has been exclusively on agriculture, public health, small business/cooperative development and engineering.

In the past, IVS volunteers worked on a wide variety of projects. For example, in Vietnam and Laos they were involved in everything from education to introducing new varieties of rice and vegetable crops. In Algeria, most volunteers taught English, while those in Madagascar tackled rural water projects. The following examples of services reflect the new IVS specialization in rural development:

Bangladesh—agricultural training, mother and child
     health care
Botswana—horticulture, village industries
Bolivia—handicraft cooperatives
Ecuador—community development, road
     construction
Papua New Guinea—small business development,
     appropriate technology
Sudan—water engineering, sheep farm management

In all of these projects, one of the essential features is the attempt by the volunteer to share with counterparts among the local population whatever skills they possess.

IVS efforts in Vietnam and Laos were greatly complicated by the war. Schools would be built and bombed out within a few weeks; new plantings of vegetables or rice would be overrun by the warring armies; community development would go by the board when the people of a village were moved to refugee camps.

Moreover, conflict between IVS and the U.S. and Vietnamese governments over the manner in which the war was conducted was a constant source of friction. Eventually, in 1971, IVS was expelled from Vietnam because of this disagreement.[13]

During the 1960s nine IVS volunteers lost their lives in Laos and Vietnam, victims of the war. The first to die was Peter Hunting. After serving a two-year term with the IVS education team in Vietnam, he volunteered to return for a second term and become a team leader. He was fully aware of the dangers awaiting him upon his return to Vietnam, particularly since as a team leader he would be required to travel extensively. A few weeks later he was shot to death by Vietcong guerrillas on a road in the Mekong Delta.

The violence of Peter's death stands in sharp contrast to the gentleness of his character. He was a man of action and a man of peace. On a scrap of paper found on his body were these thoughts:

By the way of Bethlehem, lead us, O Lord, to newness of life.
By the innocence of the Christ Child, renew our simple trust.
By the tenderness of Mary, deliver us from cruelty and hardness of hearts.
By the patience of Joseph, save us from all rash judgments and ill-tempered action.
By the shepherd's watch, open our eyes to the signs of thy coming.
By the wise men's journey, keep our searching spirits from fainting.

By the music of the heavenly choir, put to shame the
   clamor of the earth.
By the shining star, guide our feet into the way of peace.

The clamor of the earth is over for Peter Hunting.
He has found the peace he so earnestly sought.

Recruiting was never a problem with IVS during
the days when the vast majority of volunteers were
young men and women, either engaged in college
studies or recently graduated. During the war in Vietnam, IVS was considered an alternative to military
service. This was one of the factors that greatly increased the number of college men seeking positions
in IVS. Indeed, during the 1960s, approximately one of
ten applicants was accepted.

However, recruitment is now a different task. Host
institutions rightly demand qualified people whose particular skills can help meet local needs. This means that
IVS is often called upon to recruit highly specialized
technicians—for example, an agronomist with special
experience in soybeans, a rice miller or a blacksmith.
So, even with an international recruitment network,
finding the right candidate to fill a position can require
much effort.

IVS is in a very direct way a forerunner of the
Peace Corps. When the Peace Corps proposal was
being debated in Congress, Senator Humphrey and
others who knew and admired IVS argued that, since
IVS had succeeded in utilizing the dedication and skills
of volunteers, the Peace Corps should be able to do the
same. The Peace Corps is vastly larger than IVS. The
result is less effective communication between volunteers and their leaders and less flexibility in placing
volunteers in assignments of their choice.

The IVS commitment to self-help has always been uncompromising. For example, during the mid-1960s when IVS attempted to introduce new varieties of rice in Vietnam, their approach to the villagers was definitely a "soft sell." A volunteer would merely plant a rice patty to the new variety. When the villagers noted the great productivity of that rice patty, the volunteers would make available seed and other inputs necessary to grow same.

One of the most impressive illustrations of self-help I have ever observed took place between 1966 and 1969 in a village called St. Vincent, about twenty miles north of Saigon. A group of North Vietnamese refugees, led by their parish priest, had fled North Vietnam in the late 1950s. After being chased several times from settlements by the war, they eventually arrived at St. Vincent and were convinced that this would be their permanent home. When I visited them in 1966, they described plans to build concrete block homes for each family, a church and a school. One of the chief instruments for this project was a manually operated machine with which they made blocks of 90 percent mud and 10 percent cement.

The role of the IVS volunteer in this case was to procure cement for the project. When I returned for a second visit to St. Vincent in 1969, I found 100 concrete block homes completed, together with a beautiful church and school. The block-making machine was broken and the priest was grieviously ill. Nevertheless, this seemingly impossible dream had been fulfilled. It is difficult to estimate the tremendous energy that was expended by the people of this village in accomplishing this goal. The input by IVS and the U.S. government was a tiny fraction of the total resources involved in the undertaking.

Many magnificent young men and women have served as volunteers in IVS. Their counterparts from the host countries have been equally diligent and heroic. It is difficult to estimate the value of IVS efforts in the nations where they served. As indicated above, many of the economic and agricultural accomplishments made with IVS technical assistance were wiped out by war in several of these countries. Nevertheless, the human development that resulted is much more enduring.

Equally significant is the tremendous impact of the IVS experience on the life and character of the American volunteers. Most of them returned to the United States and are engaged in civilian activities. Almost without exception, they bring to their new life in the United States a humility, a degree of appreciation of human dignity and a wisdom that few other Americans possess. Many of them have risen to influential positions in government, business and the Church.

11
Integrated Development in the Caribbean

The people of the Caribbean Islands are close to us, historically, geographically and economically. The trade winds that blow gently from the Atlantic into the Caribbean brought Columbus to this part of the New World on October 12, 1493. Europeans treated the Carib Indians very badly in the ensuing years, resulting in their complete extinction. White planters brought Africans to this part of the world to tend their sugar plantations. Most of the present citizens of the Caribbean area are descendants of those original slaves. Wars between the British, Spanish, French and Dutch kept the islands of this area in constant turmoil. Then followed a period in which colonialism reigned with most of the economic and social disadvantages it embodies.[14]

During recent years the British have attempted to greatly reduce their involvement in their Caribbean colonies. Most of these former British colonies have become associate states of the empire. Since the population of these islands is so small and their resources are so limited, many economic problems have plagued them. Most of these islands are dependent on a one-crop economy. The level of education is very low. Most of the capable young men and women leave the islands seeking better opportunities elsewhere. Understandably, the political leadership of most of these islands is less than outstanding. Surely there are few places in the world where self-help and creative economic programs are more needed than here.

For these many reasons, I responded to an invitation in January 1965 to initiate a self-help program in one of the Caribbean Islands, Carriacou, which is a part of the associate state of the Grenadines. The invitation was extended to me by a classmate, the Reverend Edward Fitton, then pastor of Carriacou. As the following report will suggest, the ensuing development efforts on Carriacou illustrate well the manner in which one development effort can be supportive of another. In other words, we were able to integrate several development programs on this island.

Carriacou is located fifteen miles north of Grenada, approximately one hundred miles north of the Coast of Venezuela, and approximately six hundred miles south of the tip of Florida. The island measures approximately twelve miles north and south and thirteen miles east and west. In 1965 the population was 6,400 people, almost all of whom were black. The religion of the people of the island was almost equally divided between Catholic and Anglican. I found that there were very few able-bodied young men on the island, most of them either having gone to other countries for work or absent from the island by reason of the fact that they were manning the many small ships and schooners that ply the waters of the Caribbean. The people of Carriacou are gentle and hospitable, though very poor.

Anyone wishing to stimulate development looks

for signs among the people of a desire for change. Back in 1965 these signs were several. Poverty had not crushed the spirit of the people. Almost every family owned at least a small piece of property. No one owned more than fifty acres. A new air strip was being constructed on the island, which would make it possible for visitors to fly from Grenada to Carriacou in approximately ten minutes. Previously travel between the islands by schooner required approximately five hours. The Grenadine government had made efforts at reclaiming badly eroded hillsides on the island by planting heavy grasses and teak trees. The Madonna House Apostolate of Combermere, Canada, had established a House on Carriacou some years previously. Several young women of Madonna House had begun efforts at forming a handicraft cooperative on the island.

One of the first steps we took as this development effort unfolded was the formation of an island-wide economic development committee, controlled completely by local citizens. This committee determined whether a proposed development project was for the benefit of the people of the island or that of outsiders. Recent experience had indicated that most other nationals had exploited rather than served the local people. This committee also began to indicate priorities in development programs under consideration.

The above-mentioned handicraft cooperative began to flourish. Two young ladies, artists, came to Carriacou as volunteers to help the island craftsmen and women improve the quality of their products. Miss Jean Cappet had received training in the Rochdale type of cooperative at St. Francis Xavier Institute, Antigonish, Nova Scotia. She led an effort to educate the island people in the fundamentals of cooperative organization. Through such efforts, improvements in marketing techniques were quickly made by the members of the handicraft cooperative. Their profits were significantly improved.

It was apparent to me that this already-established educational effort in cooperation could easily serve in the formation of other cooperatives. Almost immediately we helped the farmers of the island form a cooperative that was an outgrowth of a government-controlled farm association. The chief asset of that association was a cotton gin donated by the government to the new cooperative. At that time the only means for plowing fields on the island was spade and fork. Realizing the great inefficiency of this method, I raised funds to purchase a small tractor with plow, tiller and other attachments, and gave it also to the cooperative. Two young men of Carriacou spent three weeks in Trinidad learning the essentials of tractor driving and maintenance. These two major resources, the cotton gin and the tractor, proved extremely valuable to the cooperative and its members.

The third most significant economic activity on the island is fishing. Back in 1965 the equipment of these fishermen was extremely primitive. They could not afford motors for their boats or any type of refrigeration. Their fishing gear was extremely simple and inefficient. Because of the lack of refrigeration, it became necessary for them to sell their catch before noon each day, lest it spoil. Miss Cappet joined with me in efforts to educate the fishermen concerning the fundamentals of cooperation. They were an extremely independent lot. The result was that this educational effort took more than one year. Eventually the fishermen's cooperative was formed and I made available to them a small ice-making machine, which helped to solve one of their major problems. They also cooperatively purchased fishing supplies and in this manner reduced the cost of such supplies and improved the quality of their equipment.

The ultimate success of any development effort depends largely upon the quality of education in the community concerned. With this in view, I took steps to help strengthen the small secondary school that was being conducted on Carriacou by the Anglican Church. Two volunteers, a man and his wife, spent three years on the island greatly strengthening the quality of instruction at this school. This provided a motive to leaders of the Grenadine government and certain private citizens to build and staff a larger and much more adequate secondary school.

As these various steps in development unfolded, we all realized that the most basic need was still unmet, namely, an adequate water supply during the dry months. Carriacou is a volcanic island. During the rainy season the water runs off into the sea or is absorbed into the soil. During the dry season there is inadequate water for human and animal consumption. We attempted to resolve this problem by building a water catchment lined with a heavy vinyl plastic. The plastic would prevent the seepage of the water into the soil below.

The problems that ensued are typical of problems that occur when a developing country begins to cope with major projects such as this water catchment. I made available the vinyl plastic for the water catchment and an engineer to supervise its installation. A key to the entire operation was a Caterpillar Tractor that had been brought to the island to build the above-mentioned air strip. When the engineer arrived on Carriacou for the final stage of this project, one of the native workers put brackish water into the radiator of the tractor. After two and a half hours of operation, the engine block cracked and the entire project was brought to a halt. I have indicated to the Grenadine government that I remain prepared to pursue this project further because I am convinced that it is feasible and urgently needed. In the meanwhile, inadequate management had caused a serious breakdown of the ice-making machine, further reducing the fruits of the several projects.

Our experience on Carriacou is indicative of the successes and heartbreaks that are to be expected in endeavors of this sort. Ultimate success depends upon the perseverance of local leaders and of those agencies providing outside assistance.

12
Iowa-Yucatan Partnership

During the years 1965 to 1971 I was actively engaged in the Iowa-Yucatan Partners of the Alliance Program. During the fall of 1965, leaders of Iowa and Yucatan agreed to a sister-state relationship with some support from the State Department's Alliance for Progress Program. The Partners of the Alliance Program was first initiated in 1961. Within two years, twenty-nine states of our nation had formed partnerships with states of various Latin American countries. By 1977 that number had grown to forty-six.[15] In 1970 the name of the program was changed to Partners of the Americas, reflecting the involvement of private individuals and organizations in these partnerships.

A significant feature of the partners program is its focus on the mutual help that inhabitants of developed countries as well as Third World people experience from properly planned people-to-people programs. I know, for example, that American International Voluntary Services volunteers received as much from as they contributed to the people with whom they lived in Africa and Southeast Asia. If First World people assume a patronizing attitude toward their Third World hosts, their welcome is soon withdrawn.

Yucatan is a state of Mexico, located on a peninsula jutting out into the Gulf of Mexico. It is an extremely interesting region with a rich history. About 90 percent of the people of Yucatan are Mayan Indians. Theirs is an ancient civilization. As early as 900 A.D., the Mayans were constructing fifteen-story buildings (many of which are still intact); they had devised a relatively sophisticated system of astronomy and mathematics; and their art and sculpture were comparable to that later developed in Egypt. Sometime before the arrival of Europeans in the late fifteenth century, the Mayans experienced a period of economic and cultural retrogression. Columbus found them living a primitive life in the rain forest. Today the Mayans of the villages of Yucatan live in essentially the same conditions as those which prevailed 400 years ago. Their homes are one-room thatched cottages; most of their goods are handcrafted and they pursue a subsistence type of agriculture.[16]

The Mayans are a quiet, lovable people. Very seldom is any Mayan guilty of lying, stealing or raucous behavior. Indeed we Americans can learn much from them.

Today the people of Yucatan are experiencing severe economic problems. Henequen, a plant providing coarse fiber for the manufacture of ropes, is their chief product. Competition from synthetics has badly depressed the market for henequen. Many Yucatacans are unemployed. They are experiencing severe health problems.

Precisely because the people of Iowa and Yucatan differ in so many ways, the partners program proved very enriching. Many mutually advantageous exchanges have occurred during the past decade. Many Yucatanians are very skilled in both voice and instrumental music. Some of their finer instrumentalists and vocalists toured Iowa, giving concerts in various communities. Meanwhile, the Partners of the Alliance in Iowa twice sponsored the famous Ballet Folklorico of Mexico City—partly for fund raising and as a cultural enrichment. A significant part of the Ballet Folklorico is based on the history, religion and aspirations of the Mayans. Meanwhile, the mixed-voice choir of the University of Iowa traveled in the spring of 1967 to Yucatan, sang the Easter Mass at the Cathedral of Merida and gave concerts in several other places throughout Yucatan. It is interesting to note that the young women of this University of Iowa choir were the first women to have sung at a mass in the Merida Cathedral during its 423-year history.

Each summer, approximately a dozen young people from Yucatan came to live with Iowa families and a corresponding number of Iowa youths spent part of their summer with families in Yucatan. A significant tourist business also emerged from this partnership. Yucatan is an extremely fascinating place to visit. The restored cities of Uxmal and Chichen Itza are graphic reminders of the splendor of the Mayan people a thousand years ago. The climate in Yucatan during the winter months is most pleasant.

Some practical services to the poor of Yucatan also were included in the Partners Program. Handicrafts manufactured by the women of Maxcanu were marketed by Iowa partners. Equipment and drugs were delivered to various clinics and hospitals in Yucatan and several physicians and dentists flew into the villages of Yucatan to provide medical services to those who would otherwise have lacked this care. Iowa partners also helped finance a series of apartments for low-income families in Merida, Yucatan.

One of the by-products of this partnership was the

establishment of an extension program in Yucatan, by Central College at Pella, Iowa, providing an opportunity for approximately thirty students each semester to study archeology in a region very rich in archeological data. Needless to say, Central College students were quick to respond to such an attractive opportunity.

In summary, the Partners of the Americas Program provides many opportunities to develop self-help programs. There are also gains through the people-to-people relationships fostered by this program, leading to the enrichment of the peoples of each sister state. Increased understanding among people from significantly different parts of the world is one of the several steps needed to firmly establish world peace.

13
Missionaries as Catalysts of Development

Missionaries and other church workers are emerging as the most significant catalytic agents in the war against hunger and poverty. The chief battlefields of that war are the rice paddies, the wheat fields, the factories and the market places of the Third World. In chapter 1 attention was drawn to the importance of according to the local people the initiative and control of development projects. On the other hand most of these projects would not be started unless some outside agent acted as a catalyst. Obviously if the local people already had all of the resources and motivation needed for development, that development would have occurred a long time ago. Among the proper functions of a catalyst are convening the concerned persons and creating a situation in which they simultaneously reflect on their felt needs. The process then can be guided toward an evaluation of resources available and resources lacking to bring about desired results. The outside agent may also be the contact person through whom monetary resources, technical skills and other needed outside inputs can be channeled into the project.

The strengths of missionaries and other church

workers in development are several. They outnumber all other agents of change working at the grass roots in the Third World. Possibly as many as 400,000 church-related Catholic and Protestant workers are now serving in the Third World. This completely dwarfs the representatives of the United States Agency for International Development, the specialized agencies of the United Nations and all other agents of change serving in those countries.

Missionaries deal extensively with low-income people. As we have noted in chapter 1, development that serves chiefly the already rich and powerful is regressive. Christian missionaries are committed in a very special way to alleviate the needs and restore the dignity of the poor and oppressed. This is fundamental to the teaching and example of Christ. There is a growing realization among missionaries that there is no consistency in preaching the Christian gospel to a people whose rights and dignity are being violated without any positive efforts to correct such disorders. Efforts to help the poor and oppressed in the Third World to help themselves might be considered a form of "preevangelism," the creating of a necessary condition for the effective preaching of the gospel.

The preaching of the gospel, on the other hand, frequently helps remedy moral disorders such as stealing, hatred and exploitation, which interfere with development.

Missionaries usually enjoy the trust of local people. They are seldom accused of seeking their own advantage. Generally speaking, missionaries respect the dignity, culture and social institutions of the people they serve. These are significant factors in developing true self-help programs.

Missionaries usually stay in an area for many years and are, thus, able to sustain support of a program for sufficient time to ensure that it will become both successful and viable. The average length of service of a missionary significantly exceeds that which is customary for agents of governments, educational institutions and international organizations. Moreover, most missionary efforts are conducted by religious orders and other societies, which maintain a continuity of presence and of policy, even when certain personnel changes occur.[17]

On the other hand, missionaries have weaknesses and needs that must be met if they are to do their part in promoting development in the Third World. Most missionary societies need more personnel. Missionaries are fewer in number and more advanced in age than in previous times. If they are to provide a significant new group of services, they must enlist additional personnel, particularly those who are skilled in agriculture, home economics, nutrition, transportation, and so forth. Indeed, most missionaries are more skilled in liturgy, catechetics and counseling than in the practical arts of agriculture, engineering and medicine.

A number of missionary societies do not at present accept development as a part of their responsibility. Information and discussion by persons well informed in development might help to enlist such missionaries in this effort. In the Roman Catholic Church, there has been a steady movement of ideology in the direction of serving the whole man and all men. Thus, particularly since Vatican II, the acceptability of involvement in development efforts has grown immensely among Catholic missionaries.

One of the first American churchmen to advocate

the involvement of missionaries in economic and social development was Monsignor L. G. Ligutti, who served as the executive director of the National Catholic Rural Life Conference from 1954 to 1958 and as the permanent observer of the Holy See to the Food and Agriculture Organization of the United Nations (FAO) from 1949 to 1971. Monsignor Ligutti was deeply involved in efforts to improve agriculture and other economic and social conditions in the Third World over a period of about thirty years. He emerged in the 1950s and 1960s as one of the most-respected and best-informed authorities in this field.[18]

From his extensive contact with both the needs of Third World people and the activities of missionaries, Monsignor Ligutti had a growing conviction that the missionaries could significantly increase their involvement in development and in this manner advance the welfare of the people they served and the effectiveness of their own mission activities. In 1962 Monsignor Ligutti spearheaded a program that resulted in the most thorough study ever made of the impact of missionaries and other religious workers on social and economic betterment in developing countries. The project was financed by a $403,000 Ford Foundation Grant. The project was jointly sponsored by the National Catholic Rural Life Conference and the Agricultural Missions Department of the National Council of Churches. The survey was conducted by the International Federation of Catholic Institutes for Social and Socio-Religious Research and the Institute of Social Studies. This was a joint Catholic-Protestant effort. The study was under the direction of Canon François Houtart. Case studies were made in Columbia, Brazil, Cameroun, India, Indonesia and Tanzania. Information gathered was published and made available to the mission-sending societies of both Catholic and Protestant churches.

The concrete response on the part of the Roman Catholic Church was the formation of Agrimissio, which has its headquarters in Rome and provides training to missionaries to better equip them to cope with agricultural, educational, social and other practical needs of Third World people. Many of the resource people making presentations at Agrimissio workshops and conferences are staff and officers of FAO. One of the results of these exchanges is to improve communication and cooperation among missionaries and representatives of FAO in the Third World. A substantial portion of the funds required for the operation of Agrimissio is provided by the National Catholic Rural Life Conference, (NCRLC), largely drawn from generous contributions made by the Homeland Foundation.

Pope Paul VI, in an audience on February 4, 1974, requested that I involve myself once more in the activities of the NCRLC, particularly with regard to the needs of rural people in developing nations. As I reflected on the Holy Father's request, it seemed that the best possible line of action would be to renew efforts to help missionaries increase their involvement in agricultural, home economics and other development programs. Upon my return to the United States, I shared this proposal with officers of the NCRLC and with Bishop Edward Swanstrom, then executive director of the Catholic Relief Services (CRS). All strongly approved the substance of the proposal.

On August 2, 1974, I met with members of the U.S. Catholic Mission Council and its staff at Washington, D.C., and on August 6, I spent six hours with the staff of CRS—USCC—at their New York offices, exploring the possible roles of CRS in this undertaking. A second meeting with the members of the U.S. Catholic Mission Council occurred on September 19, 1974, in Washington, D.C. On November 22, 1974, I convened in Washington, D.C., a meeting with officers and staff of the U.S. Catholic Mission Council and with the mission committees of the Leadership Conference of Women Religious and the Conference of Major Superiors of Men in the United States.

I had approached these missionary organizations presuming that their greatest need would be for missionary training similar to that offered by Agrimissio in Rome. I envisioned an American-based training center providing a similar service. However, from these several meetings it became apparent that there was already available all of the training that these missionaries needed. Leaders of these missionary organizations indicated to me that their needs were rather for more technical assistance in forming and evaluating development projects, financial assistance for such work, more lay volunteers to be added to the ecclesiastical teams in the Third World, better cooperation and communication among private and governmental agencies engaged in development efforts in the Third World and ways of bringing about better understanding by missionaries and their societies of the import of development in the total task with which they were concerned.

These conversations led logically to a series of meetings with other nongovernmental agencies engaged in development in the Third World. During the last weeks of 1974, I convened two meetings of the following organizations in New York City: CRS—USCC, U.S. Catholic Mission Council, Agricultural Missions, Cooperation in Development (CODEL) and

International Liaison. These meetings were very fruitful. Each organization learned from others how it might improve its services to missionaries engaged in development and relate those efforts more closely to those of other organizations.

This effort climaxed on May 15, 1975, with the convening of a very large group of nongovernmental agencies and their personnel. In attendance at the meeting were thirty-one representatives of the following organizations: CRS, Church World Servides, Lutheran World Relief, United Methodist Committee on Relief, CODEL, U.S. Catholic Mission Council, Agricultural Missions, International Liaison, Maryknoll Fathers, Technoserve, Institute for Study and Application of Integrated Development, Global Education Associates, World Brotherhood Exchange, Maryknoll Sisters and Holy Ghost Fathers.

By this time it became apparent that CODEL was the one agency that might most effectively serve the needs about which we had been speaking for so many months. CODEL, formed in 1969, is a consortium of thirty-nine church-related Catholic and Protestant organizations engaged in missionary, development or relief activities in the Third World. CODEL helps develop self-help projects, provides high-caliber technical assistance to projects in progress and assists in the evaluation of projects as they progress. It is also an instrument through which information and cooperation among the parent organizations can be increased as they serve in the Third World. At about the time of the May 15, 1975, meeting, CODEL had just received an $860,000 USAID grant to support and test development projects in the Third World. One of the chief conclusions of that meeting, therefore, was the resolve by the parent organizations belonging to CODEL to use its services more effectively.[19] In addition, a number of mission-sending societies continued to show interest in increased availability of technically competent volunteers to assist on their missionary teams. International Liaison for Volunteer Lay Ministers of Washington, D.C., is committed to the task of enlisting such volunteers, preparing dossiers of their qualifications and forwarding information to interested missionary and other organizations. In the Roman Catholic Church, the U.S. Catholic Mission Council will continue to serve as one of the chief instruments for bringing about an increased awareness on the part of Catholic missionaries of their potential roles as catalysts for development.

In my estimation, the stage is set for a major breakthrough in development efforts in the Third World. Month by month there is a growing awareness on the part of missionaries of their possible roles in development and an increased number of successful experiences in this regard. A current illustration of such a successful project is that in which the Maryknoll Fathers are engaged in the eastern lowland jungles of Bolivia near the town of Mineros, which is eighty kilometers north of the city of Santa Cruz. The population of the area is estimated at sixty thousand, 95 percent of whom are poor farmers. They live in a land area of approximately fifty thousand acres, most of which has been given by the government to individual farmers in fifty-acre plots. The climate is tropical and the land is very fertile. However, working by hand, the small farmer can work only about two acres of land, typically planted in rice and corn, which is barely enough to eke out an existence.

A cooperative, Mineros Cooperative, has been

formed to amalgamate and unify the common cause of these poor farmers, thus making it possible for them to clear and work more of the land area. Each farmer donates $2.50 (approximately 5 percent of his family income) and his labor to clear ninety acres of jungle by hand. Examination of the results of the pilot program in this undertaking indicated that this was indeed a project worth supporting.

However, despite the selfless labor of the farmers and leadership of Maryknoll Fathers such as Father Douglas Coneely, the jungle grows faster than it can be cleared by hand. Literally, the jungle's second growth has overtaken the agricultural process in many instances before the fields could be planted.

At this point, Father Coneely appealed to me and other members of the Mission Commission of the diocese of Peoria for assistance. After careful deliberation, we decided to provide $52,000 together with $26,000 offered by the Maryknoll Fathers, which permitted the purchase of a D7 Caterpillar Tractor and a Rome KJ Clearing Blade. Our $52,000 was contributed by many hundreds of interested Catholics in our diocese. Early in March 1977, the tractor and the clearing blade were delivered at Mineros and immediately employed to assist the farmers in clearing their land and keeping back the second growth. Thus the generosity of the Catholics of the Peoria Diocese plus the tremendous diligence and energy of the farmers of Mineros have combined into a truly great leap forward in this important project. Without the leadership of the Maryknoll Fathers, this entire undertaking would never have occurred.

There seems at this time to be an increasing interest on the part of the federal government, foundations and private business to lend financial assistance to missionaries engaged in self-help projects in the Third World.

Self-help is an extremely difficult task. However, it seems at long last that the leadership required to make such projects effective and enduring is being marshaled. The result may well be a significant improvement in the economic and social conditions of the most impoverished people of the Third World, together with a growing acceptability and effectiveness of the Catholic and Protestant missionaries who serve in those countries.

14
New and Future Types of Self-Help

The self-help projects described in previous chapters are efforts by communities to improve their economic, educational or social conditions. New types of self-help are now surfacing in which individual needs are served.

The best-known program of this type is Alcoholics Anonymous (AA). Since several other programs are patterned after AA, let us examine it in some detail.

Alcoholics Anonymous was initiated by a New York businessman in 1935 while on a visit to Akron, Ohio. Four years later the movement acquired its name (Alcoholics Anonymous) from the title of a book published on the subject. Today approximately one million men and women follow the practices of AA.

The AA General Service Conference describes this movement as follows:[20]

What Is A.A.?

Alcoholics Anonymous is a worldwide fellowship of men and women who help each other to stay sober. They offer the same help to anyone who has a drinking problem and wants to do something about it. Since they are all alcoholics themselves, they have a special understanding of each other. They know what the illness feels like—and they have learned how to recover from it in AA.

An AA member says, "I am an alcoholic"—even when he has not had a drink for many years. He does not say that he is "cured." Once a person has lost the ability to control his drinking, this AA would explain, he can never again manage to drink safely—or, in other words, he can never become "a former alcoholic" or "an ex-alcoholic." But in AA he can become a sober alcoholic, a recovered alcoholic.

How Does AA Help the Alcoholic?

Through the example and friendship of the recovered alcoholics in AA, the new member is encouraged to stay away from a drink "one day at a time," as they do. Instead of "swearing off forever" or worrying about whether he will be sober tomorrow, the alcoholic concentrates on not drinking right now—today.

By keeping alcohol out of his system, the newcomer takes care of one part of his illness—his body has a chance to get well. But remember, there is another part. If he is going to stay sober, he needs a healthy mind and healthy emotions, too. So he begins to straighten out his confused thinking and unhappy feelings by following AA's "Twelve Steps" to recovery. These Steps suggest ideas and actions that can guide him toward a happy and useful life.

To be in touch with other members and to learn about the recovery program, the new member goes to AA meetings regularly.

What Are AA Meetings?

Alcoholics Anonymous is made up of almost 30,000 local groups, in 92 countries. The people in each group get together, usually once or twice a week, to hold AA meetings, of two main types:

1. At "open meetings," speakers tell how they drank, how they discovered AA and how its program has helped them. Members may bring relatives or friends, and usually anyone interested in AA is also welcome to attend "open meetings."

2. "Closed meetings" are for alcoholics only. These are group discussions, and any member who wants to may speak up, to ask questions and to share his thoughts with his fellow members. At "closed meetings," each AA can get help with his personal problems in staying sober and in everyday living. Some other AA will have had the same problems and can explain how he handled them—often by using one or more of the Twelve Steps.

Who Belongs to AA?

Like other illnesses, alcoholism strikes all sorts of people. So the men and women in AA are of all races and nationalities, all religions and no religion at all. They are rich and poor and just average. They work at all occupations, as lawyers and housewives, teachers and truck drivers, waitresses and clergymen.

AA does not keep a list of members, but groups do report how many people belong to each one. From these reports, total AA membership is estimated at over 1,000,000.

The "Twelve Steps" are basic to the AA program. They are as follows:

1. We admitted we were powerless over alcohol—that our lives had become unmanageable.

2. Came to believe that a Power greater than ourselves could restore us to sanity.

3. Made a decision to turn our will and our lives over to the care of God *as we understood Him*.

4. Made a searching and fearless moral inventory of ourselves.

5. Admitted to God, to ourselves and to another human being the exact nature of our wrongs.

6. Were entirely ready to have God remove all these defects of character.

7. Humbly asked Him to remove our shortcomings.

8. Made a list of all persons we had harmed and became willing to make amends to them all.

9. Made direct amends to such people wherever possible, except when to do so would injure them or others.

10. Continued to take personal inventory and when we were wrong promptly admitted it.

11. Sought through prayer and meditation to improve our conscious contact with God as we understood Him, praying only for knowledge of His will for us and the power to carry that out.

12. Having had a spiritual awakening as the result of these steps, we tried to carry this message to alcoholics, and to practice these principles in all our affairs.

Is AA a Religious Society?

AA is not a religious society since it requires no definite religious belief as a condition of membership. Although it has been endorsed and approved by many religious leaders, it is not allied with any organization or sect. Included in its membership are Catholics, Protestants, Jews, members of other major religious bodies, agnostics and atheists.

The AA program of recovery from alcoholism is undeniably based on acceptance of certain spiritual values. The individual member is free to interpret those values as he thinks best, or not to think about them at all, if he so elects.

Before he turned to AA, the average alcoholic had already admitted that he could not control his drinking. Alcohol had, for him, become a power greater than himself, and it had been accepted in those terms. AA suggests that, to achieve and maintain sobriety, the alcoholic needs to accept and depend upon another Power that he recognizes is greater than himself. Some alcoholics choose to consider the AA group itself as the power greater than themselves; for many others, this Power is God—as they, individually, understand Him; still others rely upon entirely different concepts of a Higher Power.

Some alcoholics when they first turn to AA, have definite reservations about accepting any concept of a Power greater than themselves. Experience shows that, if they will keep an open mind on the subject and keep coming to AA meetings, they are not likely to have too difficult a time in working out an acceptable solution to this distinctly personal problem.

Al-Anon and Alateen are self-help organizations closely related to AA. Al-Anon is a group of wives, husbands, and other relatives and friends of alcoholics. It is a group of sympathetic persons who have firsthand knowledge of the problems of living with an alcoholic. Group discussions help relieve the constant emotional strains and pressures, and make it possible for the relative to better help the alcoholic. It is not necessary to wait for the alcoholic to join Alcoholics Anonymous before joining Al-Anon. Alateen groups are made up of teenagers with a parent or parents who are problem drinkers. The teenagers run the meetings themselves, though each group has a sponsor who is a member of Al-Anon. Discussions focus on the nature and cause of alcoholism, and on dealing with the resentment and self-pity that arise in children of alcoholics.

The great success of AA has prompted other groups with common problems or aspirations to band together and follow similar policies. Persons with drug addiction are banding together in an organization almost identical with that of AA. Divorced Fathers is a self-help organization of men who have been divorced by their wives or are threatened with divorce. Parents Anonymous is a crisis-intervention program whose primary objective is to help prevent damaging relationships between parents and their children. As in AA, weekly group meetings are held by Parents Anonymous. In many cities Parents Anonymous maintains a twenty-four hour answering service to provide counsel to parents who are fearful that they may injure their children.

Let us turn our attention now to directions self-help programs may take in the future. In my estimation the most dramatic innovations will be found in our cities. In chapter 9, I observed that self-help has not thrived in U.S. cities and that many urban self-help programs are largely political in their objectives. Instead of creating significant new goods and services, they are largely ways to force governmental officials and others to respond more effectively to the needs and rights of the urban poor. Consequently, it appears that our cities are most in need of self-help initiatives.

The focal point of such initiatives must be the neighborhood. Urban residents identify with neighborhoods, not the entire city. Most cities are too vast to be a functional unit for self-help efforts.

During the past five years awareness of the rights and needs of white ethnic groups has emerged. Perhaps this will set the stage for more effective self-help. Common bonds among participants is a strong asset in self-help programs. Many of the white ethnics who remain in our cities have incomes in the lower-middle bracket. They are largely bypassed by most antipoverty and social legislation. As they become more conscious of their rights and needs, with the right leadership, significant self-help efforts are likely to emerge. One of the most effective of the organizations providing such leadership among urban dwellers is the National Center for Urban Ethnic Affairs (NCUEA), 1521 Sixteenth St., N. W., Washington, D.C. 20036. NCUEA, founded in 1970 by Monsignor Geno C. Baroni, is helping white ethnics focus on their own heritage and cultural identity and providing capital and technical assistance as they band together to help themselves.

The major objective of NCUEA is to bring about better understanding and more cooperation among urban blacks, Chicanos and white ethnics. The Organization for Neighborhood Development Inc. (ONDI) is the agency through which NCUEA assists in the revitalization and economic development of urban neighborhoods. ONDI attracts significant financial support from the Small Business Administration and the National Development Council. As of 1977 sixty local development companies had been established in eleven selected cities and had generated $31,500,000 in pending and finalized loans.

Another subsidiary of NCUEA is the Catholic Conference on Ethnic and Neighborhood Affairs (CCENA), which was formed in 1974 and is affiliated with the U.S. Catholic Conference in Washington, D.C. CCENA helps build organizations on the parish level. Parochial response has been so great that CCENA has developed files on fifty cities, which document activities in over fifty neighborhoods and parishes. Staff has visited twenty-three of these cities during the years 1974–1977 and local CCENA programs have been developed in over a dozen cities. Subgrants of $30,000 each to four cities have leveraged $224,250 from other local, private and public sources.

The "farm strike" launched in December 1977 is a reminder that the agricultural industry is repeatedly faced with a price-cost squeeze that often results in losses rather than income for the majority of our farmers. In the past, efforts at industry-wide collective bargaining by farmers have failed. Nevertheless, such a program will repeatedly surface until American farmers gain more control over the prices they receive for produce and the prices they pay for fuel, fertilizer, seed, and other items needed to produce their crops and livestock.

I predict that as more people in every walk of life become aware of the effectiveness of the self-help approach, a great variety of new self-help initiatives will emerge. In my estimation this will represent new hope for a just and viable economy and social order both in the United States and in the Third World.

15
The Task Ahead

This is the story of disadvantaged people—at home and abroad—uniting to lift themselves from poverty and to regain self-esteem and dignity. Recorded in this book are the heroic efforts of men and women of uncommon character and courage. This is largely a story of success, pointing to the possibility of even greater progress toward these goals if the principles of self-help are more widely employed.

The prominence of religious leaders and their organizations in these accounts is not accidental. Concern for the dignity of individuals and the resolve to assist poor and powerless people are very basic to religions, particularly to Christianity. In chapter 13 I suggest that missionaries and other church workers are the most promising source of leadership in self-help programs in the Third World. This increasing involvement of church workers in development reflects a new emphasis on service in practical affairs, which is now evident in most Christian communions. Vatican Council II gave special impetus to this trend in the Roman Catholic Church.

Self-help is the common denominator of each of the programs described in the preceding chapters. Yet these programs illustrate other closely related features of man's struggle for dignity and independence.

Cooperatives are the most frequently employed structures for economic self-help. They are the mainstay of self-help efforts by the blacks of the South, the poor of Appalachia and the people of Carriacou. The most dramatic self-help effort described in this book is the struggle of farm workers in California to establish their union. The Iowa-Yucatan Partnership is, first and foremost, a people-to-people program, resulting in improved economic, social and cultural experiences for the people of each of the sister states. More importantly, people of each state learn to respect the culture and traditions of the other people. This respect for a foreign culture is a key to effective self-help in the Third World as is impressively illustrated in the description of International Voluntary Services in chapter 10.

Ownership of productive property is a logical sequel to participation in co-ops, as illustrated in chapter 4. When members of an entire rural community resolve to help themselves, industrial development, agricultural improvements, educational expansion and better merchandizing are the order of the day.

This rapid overview of self-help in greatly different economies and cultures forces us to conclude that the self-help technique will work anywhere, if the basic principles of self-help described in chapter 1 are observed. For example, in Peoria, Illinois, today, community-wide efforts at urban renewal are taking place. A significant part of that renewal is the activity of several self-help organizations, including the Northside Action Council, the Southside Improvement Association, Common Place Community and the Moss-Bradley Home Owners Association.

Religious and other nongovernmental organizations are the agencies chiefly responsible for the self-help programs described in this book. Still, in many instances, governmental agencies of the United States and of the host nations have been involved. I am of the opinion that, with rare exceptions, governmental agencies are not suited to organize self-help programs. More appropriately, they should provide financial and other support to the nongovernmental organizations serving as catalysts of self-help at the grass roots.

Sadly, I also note that incompetent and corrupt governments in the Third World are the chief obstacles to self-help and development. Conversely, self-help programs aid in the creation of the type of initiative and self-determination at the grass roots that is the ultimate foundation from which better governments can emerge.

World peace is gravely endangered by the extreme gap in the standards of living prevailing in the Third World and those found in the industrialized world. Self-help programs must be an increasing part of our response to this problem. Such programs release a tremendous amount of energy and local resources. They are usually enduring; they help remedy the bitterness, hopelessness and frustration usually found among the world's poor and powerless.

The purpose, therefore, of this book is to remind all involved in antipoverty programs at home and development programs abroad of the requirements of self-help. It is my hope that such programs will expand and that the quality of such programs will be improved in light of the experiences of many thousands of people who have engaged in self-help programs during these past twenty years.

Recommended Organizations

The preceding chapters present a challenge. These organizations are helping the poor and powerless help themselves. Your response may be a desire to volunteer your services or your financial support to one or more of the following:

Southern Cooperative Development Fund, Inc., Box 3885, Lafayette, La. 70501.

Commission on Religion in Appalachia, 864 Weisgarber Road, N.W., Knoxville, Tenn. 37919.

United Farm Workers of America, AFL-CIO, La Paz, Keene, Calif. 93531.

Southwest Indian Foundation, 308 E. Hill, Gallup, N. Mex. 87301.

International Voluntary Services, Inc., Suite 605, 1717 Massachusetts Ave., N.W., Washington, D.C. 20036.

United States Catholic Mission Council, Suite 702, 1302 Eighteenth St., N.W., Washington, D.C., 20036.

Campaign For Human Development, 1312 Massachusetts Ave., N.W., Washington, D.C. 20005.

Bibliography

Abelson, Philip H., ed. *Food-Politics, Economics, Nutrition and Research*. Washington, D.C.: American Association for the Advancement of Science, 1975.

Brown, Dee. *Bury My Heart at Wounded Knee*. New York: Holt, Rinehart & Winston, 1970.

Buhlmann, Walbert. *The Coming of the Third Church*. Maryknoll, N.Y.: Orbis, 1977.

Cogswell, James A., ed. *The Church and the Rural Poor*. Atlanta: John Knox Press, 1975.

Caudill, Harry N. *Night Comes to the Cumberlands*. New York: Little Brown, 1963.

Dunn, Richard. *Sugar and Slaves: The Rise of the Planter Class in the English West Indies*. New York: Morton, 1972.

Foster, George M. *Traditional Societies and Technological Change*. New York: Harper & Row, 1973.

Gutierrez, Gustavo. *A Theology of Liberation*. New York: Maryknoll, 1973.

Harrington, Michael, and Jacobs, Paul, eds. *Labor in a Free Society*. Berkeley: University of California Press, 1959.

Kawai, Kazuro. *Japan's American Interlude*. University of Chicago Press, 1960.

Kelso, Louis, and Adler, Mortimer. *The New Capitalists*. New York: Random House, 1961.

Kiesberg, Martin, and Steele, Howard. *Improving Market Systems in Developing Countries*. Foreign Agricultural Economics Report 93. Washington, D.C.: U.S. Research Service, USDA, 1972.

Lederer, William, and Burdick, Eugene. *The Ugly American*. New York: Fawcett, 1958.

Luce, Don, and Sommer, John. *Viet Nam—The Unheard Voices*. Ithaca, N.Y.: Cornell University Press, 1969.

Miller, Ed Mack. *Maryknoll—At Work in the World*. New York: Maryknoll Fathers, 1974.

Moore, Truman. *The Slaves We Rent*. New York: Random House, 1965.

National Center for Community Action. *Human Work for Human Needs—A Catalogue of Community Action Programs*. Washington, D.C., 1975.

Sommer, John G. *Beyond Charity*. Washington, D.C.: Overseas Development Council, 1977.

Taylor, Ronald. *Chavez and the Farm Workers*. Boston: Beacon, 1975.

Thompson, John E.S. *Maya History and Religion*. Norman: University of Oklahoma Press, 1970.

Todd, Paul. *The Marshall Plan*. Washington, D.C.: Economic Cooperation Administration, 1950.

Ulman, Lloyd. *The Rise of the National Trade Union*. Cambridge: Harvard University Press, 1966.

Voorhis, J.J. *American Cooperatives: Where They Come From; What They Do; Where They Are Going*. New York: Harper, 1961.

Weller, Jack. *Yesterday's People*. Lexington: University of Kentucky Press, 1965.

Williams, Eric E. *From Columbus to Castro: The History of the Caribbean*. New York: Harper & Row, 1970.

Yzermans, Vincent. *The People I Love*. Collegeville, Minn.: Liturgical Press, 1976.

Notes

1. Jerry Voorhis is an outstanding leader of the cooperative movement in the United States. For a brief history of that movement, see his *American Cooperatives: Where They Come From; What They Do; Where They Are Going* (New York: Harper, 1961).

2. For more information about the rationale and history of labor unions, see Lloyd Ulman, *The Rise of the National Trade Union* (Cambridge: Harvard University Press, 1966) and Michael Harrington and Paul Jacobs, eds., *Labor in a Free Society* (Berkeley: University of California Press, 1959).

3. U.S. involvement in postwar reconstruction in Japan is reported in depth by Kazuro Kawai in *Japan's American Interlude* (University of Chicago Press, 1960); regarding the reconstruction of Western Europe, see Paul Todd, *The Marshall Plan* (Washington, D.C.: Economic Cooperation Administration, 1950).

4. An up-to-date and thorough treatise on the relative effectiveness of relief as compared to development and self-help is presented by John G. Sommer in his *Beyond Charity* (Washington, D.C.: Overseas Development Council, 1977).

5. Matthew 25:31–46.

6. Reporting on intermediate technology in practice is Philip H. Abelson, ed., *Food-Politics, Economics, Nutrition and Research* (Washington, D.C.: American Association for the Advancement of Science, 1975).

7. The exploitation of resources and people in Appalachia is recorded in Harry Caudill, *Night Comes to the Cumberlands* (New York: Little, 1963), and Jack Weller, *Yesterday's People* (Lexington: University of Kentucky Press, 1965).

9. A classic treatise of the bearing of ownership on income is Louis Kelso and Mortimer Adler, *The New Capitalists* (New York: Random House, 1961).

10. For more information concerning Community Action Committees see *Human Work for Human Needs, A Catalogue of Community Action Programs*, by the staff of the National Center for Community Action (Washington, D.C.: 1975).

11. Readable and reliable is Ronald Taylor, *Chavez and the Farm Workers* (Boston: Beacon, 1975).

12. For a popular record of white-Indian conflicts, see Dee Brown, *Bury My Heart at Wounded Knee* (New York: Holt, Rinehart & Winston, 1970).

13. Don Luce and John Sommers, IVS volunteers who served in Vietnam during the war years, report on the tragic impact of the war on the Vietnamese people in *Viet Nam — The Unheard Voices* (Ithaca: Cornell University Press, 1969).

14. The impact of exploitation of resources, slavery and colonialism on the people of the West Indies is reported in Eric E. Williams, *From Columbus to Castro: The History of the Caribbean* (New York: Harper & Row, 1970); for a more popular treatise, see Richard Dunn, *Sugar and Slaves* (New York: Morton, 1972).

15. These 46 partnerships match states in the United States with states, regions or countries in Latin America. Alabama-Guatemala; Arkansas-East Bolivia; California-Baja California, Sinaloa, Morelos, Nayarit, Mexico; Colorado-Minas Gerais, Brazil; Connecticut-Paraiba, Brazil; Delaware-Panama; District of Columbia-Brasilia, Brazil; Florida-Northern and Central Colombia; Georgia-Pernambuco, Brazil; Idaho-Mountain region, Ecuador; Illinois-Sao Paulo, Brazil; Indiana-Rio Grande do Sul, Brazil; Iowa-Yucatan Peninsula, Mexico; Kansas-Paraguay; Kentucky-Highlands, Ecudaor; Louisiana-El Salvador; Maine-Rio Grande do Norte, Brazil; Maryland-Rio de Janeiro, Brazil; Massachusetts-Antioquia, Colombia; Michigan-Belize and Dominican Republic; Minnesota-Uruguay; Missouri-Para, Brazil; Nebraska-Piaui, Brazil; New Hampshire-Ceara, Brazil; New Jersey-Alagoas, Brazil; New Mexico-Tabasco, Michoacan, Mexico; New York (Capital Area)-Barbados; New York (Central)-Trinidad and Tobago; New York (Western)-Jamaica; North Carolina-Cochabamba, Bolivia; Ohio-Parana, Brazil; Oklahoma-Chihuahua, Coahuila, Colima, Jalisco, Puebla, Sonora, and Tlaxcala, Mexico; Oregon-Costa Rica; Pennsylvania-Bahia,

Brazil; Rhode Island-Sergipe, Brazil; San Francisco Bay Area-Mexico City, Mexico; South Carolina-Southwestern Colombia; Tennessee-Amazonas, Brazil, and Venezuela; Texas-Peru; Utah-La Paz and Altiplano, Bolivia; Vermont-Honduras; Virginia-Santa Catarina, Brazil; Washington-Guayas and Los Rios, Ecuador; West Virginia-Espirito Santo, Brazil; Wisconsin-Nicaragua; Wyoming-Goias, Brazil.

16. Much has been written about Mayan history, culture and religion. One of the better treatises is John E.E. Thompson, *Maya History and Religion* (Norman, University of Oklahoma Press, 1970).

17. For an up-to-date report on the involvement of missionaries in Third World development, see Walbert Buhlmann, *The Coming of the Third Church* (Maryknoll, N.Y.: Orbis, 1977). The part played in this new thrust by Maryknoll missionaries is recorded in Ed Mack Miller, *Maryknoll—At Work in the World* (New York: Maryknoll, 1974). The theology behind this movement is presented in the somewhat controversial *A Theology of Liberation* by Gustavo Gutierrez (New York: Maryknoll, 1973).

18. Monsignor Ligutti's contribution to development in the Third World is included in his biography, *The People I Love*, by Vincent Yzermans (Collegeville, Minn.: Liturgical Press, 1976).

19. For more information about CODEL, write to their headquarters at 79 Madison Avenue, New York, N.Y. 10016.

20. From *A Brief Guide to Alcoholics Anonymous* (1972), *44 Questions* (1952) and *Twelve Steps* (1952), copyright by Alcoholics Anonymous World Services, Inc. Reprinted by permission of Alcoholics Anonymous World Services, Inc.